A CONNOISSEUR'S GUIDE TO ANTIQUE

CLOCKS & WATCHES

A CONNOISSEUR'S GUIDE TO ANTIQUE
CLOCKS & WATCHES

RONALD PEARSALL

TIGER

This edition published in 1997 by
Tiger Books International PLC, Twickenham

This book was designed and produced by
Todtri Productions Limited P.O. Box 572, New York,
NY 10116-0572 FAX: (212) 279-1241

Printed and bound in Singapore

ISBN 1-85501-ADD

CONTENTS

INTRODUCTION

Opposite: An ornate ormolu and porcelain striking mantel clock of the Louis Philippe (1773–1850) period. The maker is Lagarde of Paris, and the figures are set on an ornamental white band rather than in circular roundels.

Below: A collection of high-quality gold watches, mainly English, the one on the top left engraved, "Viner & Co / Inventors / 233 Regent Street", and around the inner rim, "Royal Exch / London". It also has a table with the title, "East of Greenwich", giving the times of various towns and cities in the British Isles and Europe. The cities are: Paris, Boulogne, Ostend, Hamburg, and Brussells (sic). As the British cities are west of Greenwich, the legend is mysterious.

What could be more companionable than the steady tick of a clock? Alas, since World War II and the takeover by electric and quartz movements, it is becoming less common, except among the legions of clock collectors. Antique clocks have never been more popular, and because millions have been produced, especially in the nineteenth century, they are still available at modest prices to those on the smallest of budgets.

The story of the clock is the story of technology. The clockmakers and the gunmakers created a new age. Once they invented the spring, working in metal was never the same again. The watchmakers invented miniaturisation. In a space sometimes no bigger than a copper coin they developed a secret world of tiny moving parts crafted by hand.

It is a tale of progress and innovation without parallel in any of the applied arts. The makers created objects of astonishing beauty and intricacy, and we can do more than simply admire antique clocks and watches—we can buy them.

CHAPTER ONE

FROM SAND CLOCK TO LANTERN CLOCK

In primitive societies men and women arose with the light and went to sleep when it got dark, but as civilization arrived it was necessary to divide time into manageable portions. Various ways evolved to measure the passing of time, some more long-lasting than others. The hourglass or sandglass allowed a trickle of sand to fall from one transparent holder to an identical one beneath, with a known time for the length of the process. If only one glass was used it was inverted at the end of the action, to start again. Sometimes sandglass clocks were used in a series, to extend the length of time measured without having to turn the clock over. As late as the nineteenth century medical practitioners carried with them sandglasses of a minute and a half duration to measure a patient's pulse. Basic as it was, the sandglass was considerably more accurate than the early clockwork timepieces, as was, indeed, almost everything, including one of the oldest, the water clock.

The oil lamp clock was not widely used, but it had the advantage of giving light as well as telling the time. The oil clock's mount, often of pewter, was marked with divisions to show the passage of the hours as the lamp burned and the oil level fell. Candles could also be marked out, but this method was not reliable because the melting of the wax around the wick was not regular.

Sundials

The most famous alternative to the clock was the sundial, made in many forms and often of great complexity, though all based on the principle of a metal stylus marking out a shadow as the sun passes through the sky. In 1612 one learned book devoted eight hundred pages to the subject of sundials. The most famous are those on columns in churchyards or on the front of churches, and one at Kirkdale Church in Yorkshire dates back to Saxon times. Freestanding sundials were sometimes engraved with additional dials showing the time at other places throughout the world. The pillar or column sundial has elliptical divisions on the upright; the shadow is provided by a stylus or gnomon on the top, often in the form of a dragon or other fabulous beast with the tail providing the actual pointer.

The use of the sundial was limited to the amount of light available, if any, and this limitation was even more applicable to the moondial. Despite its manifest inadequacies, the sundial was made in large quantities in pocket form from the seventeenth century, often hinged and containing a compass and complicated tables. The stylus was often replaced by a thin silk cord that could be moved so that the dial (always

Opposite: An hour glass of the seventeenth century, with barley-sugar twist uprights, and a circular base and top enlivened with quality turning. Hour glasses were still in common use, and were often better timekeepers than the clocks of the 1600s. They were decorative and were displayed even when not in use. Portable hour glasses were used well into the nineteenth century by doctors on their calls.

Above: A primitive water clock from about 1415 B.C., from Karnak, a village in central Egypt on the site of the ancient city of Thebes. Water clocks were of various forms, and this bowl would have received the water from the working mechanism of the clock. Karnak is the site of a great temple, and the area was a centre of high civilization.

Right: The remains of the Tower of Winds, a great water clock of Andronikos of Cyrrhus in Greece, dating from the first century B.C. The tower is more correctly known as a horologium. It is octagonal, with figures carved on each side representing the eight principal winds.

Opposite: Dating from 1493, this magnificent sundial from Strasburg cathedral is more a work of art than a simple method of finding out the time. An inventive feature is the shape of the hour face and the extraordinary modernistic quality of the numbers, similar in style to Art Nouveau, though the clock pre-dates that movement by four-hundred years.

Previous page: A twelfth-century sundial from North Stoke, England, set in the church tower. The dial has a few unique features, such as the head of a figure, perhaps the priest, which acts as the stylus, and the hands gripping the sundial.

Above: The earliest mechanical clock is the turret clock in Salisbury Cathedral, dating from 1386. Though it has been altered over the years, this iron caged creation established the basics of clockmaking: the motive power provided by weights wound round a revolving drum, and toothed wheels to interrupt this power. Unfortunately, the makers of this clock are unknown.

Opposite: By the third millenium B.C., Chinese astronomers discovered that equinoxes and solstices could be determined by observation of the stars. Astronomy was introduced into Europe when a school was founded on the island of Cos in the eastern Mediterranean in 640 B.C. The Arabs were the most important astronomers, and their findings reached Europe via the Moors of Spain. Britain finally assumed a role in the thirteenth century, due to the efforts of John Holywood, known as Sacro Bosco (died 1256), who wrote Sphaera Mundi, an astronomical textbook which went through fifty-nine editions. The astronomical clock of Wells Cathedral dates from this period, a beautiful work of art but of little practical use.

called a dial, never a sundial) could be used at other lattitudes. Pocket dials were luxury objects made of costly materials, and because they were of limited use they must be reckoned as no more than fashionable gadgets, especially since more or less reliable clocks were appearing indoors, coexisting with the great age of the pocket dial.

Early Mechanical Clocks

The first mechanical clocks were great structures of iron wheels that were mounted in open frames of forged iron on the bell towers of churches or similar buildings to sound the hours. Known as turret clocks, they were driven by weights suspended inside the towers. The weights were hung on ropes wound around wooden drums linked by a ratchet mechanism with the first toothed wheel of the clock movement. The earliest records of such clocks date back to the thirteenth century in Europe. Already a close association was evident between the craftsman and applied science; in clockmakers and gunmakers we see the future of civilization.

The earliest extant turret clock is that in Salisbury Cathedral, provisionally dated at 1386, though much altered since; the clock at Dover Castle is perhaps more authentic. The clock that sounds the quarters at Rouen dates from 1389. Rough and ready as the turret clock was, all the basic ingredients of the successful clock can be seen—the use of gravity to activate a train of toothed wheels, and the need to interrupt the descending weights, to provide, as it were, the "tick tock" that would not fully arrive for some considerable time. The other device that needed to be invented for motive power was the spring, and this came from the gunmakers.

The first domestic clocks were small-scale turret clocks. The wheelwork was mounted in a four-posted iron cage resting on a stand or more usually a wall brack-

et, with the weights dangling below and a bell or bells above, usually within a spire or dome. Much made in Germany and Austria in the fifteenth and sixteenth centuries, these Gothic clocks—though visually spectacular—were not particularly accurate. Yet they served their purpose, since precise timekeeping was not necessary except in navigation (where it did not arrive until the Harrison chronometer of 1772) and until the arrival of the railways in the nineteenth century.

The Gothic clock was followed in the seventeenth century by the similar but more refined lantern clock; the main difference was that the lantern clock was of brass rather than iron. The lantern clock was so called because it was the shape of a lantern of the period, with a gentle domed open-frame hood. Spring-driven clocks appeared in the second half of the fifteenth century, and although springs might have seemed to answer all time-keeping problems there was the annoying feature that spring was released at an uneven speed as the tension eased.

The answer was to wind the spring around a conical centre—the fusee, which acted as an equalising gear, compensating for the unequal rate of unwinding. Developed at an early stage in spring-driven clocks, the fusee was retained in high-quality English clocks and is often a guarantee of superiority. Whereas the interior of a clock may present a scene of great confusion and complexity to the uninitiated, a fusee can immediately be recognised.

It might be supposed that a table clock is any clock that would suitably appear on a table, but technically the term applies to a sixteenth- or seventeenth-century spring-driven clock in a gilt metal case. Largely German and French in inspiration,

Right: A graphic representation of the working of a water clock from an illuminated manuscript. An analogy may be drawn between a water clock and a water mill, and a water mill could be adapted, if one were so inclined, to telling the time, provided that the supply of water was constant.

Opposite: Astronomical clock by So Sung of about 1088 A.D. During this period, Chinese astronomy was three centuries ahead of western astronomy, and it was not until the seventeenth century, when Jesuit missionaries informed the Chinese of the discoveries of Copernicus, that Chinese astronomy was superseded. Several astronomical clocks of the period of the So Sung clock were discovered in Peking (Beijing) in 1881 when China was being routinely invaded and looted; no doubt their survival was due to the fact that they could not be eaten, easily sold, or raped.

Right: A spectacular twenty-four hour and astronomical clock on the clock tower in Berne, Switzerland, dating from about 1530. It has a ring depicting the signs of the zodiac, with figures and animals that perform at the appropriate time, (usually every hour and sometimes on the quarter in such clocks). Clocks with moving figures were once common. Many were made in Britain in the Victorian period as examples of civic pride, but this did not stop them being scrapped after World War II.

*Right: A standing south German clock of
about 1675. Details include a clock with
two subsidiary dials and an astronomical
clock, the wood ebonised walnut, the fittings
of silver and silver gilt with realistic figures
in alcoves and a main statue of Atlas. The
maker of this magnificent clock is unknown.*

*Opposite: The name "table clock" was given
to gilt clocks of the sixteenth and seventeenth century, many of which had the dial
on the top and were supplied with touch
pins so that the time could be found in the
dark. Endless invention was devoted to the
design of the cases, and some might be
described as mystery clocks, as in the
Crucifixion clock. Table clocks were not
especially accurate; the cases were far more
important than the somewhat routine
spring-driven movements.*

table clocks were often drumlike in shape, with the dial lying horizontally or positioned vertically. Sometimes touch pins were provided by the hour numerals so that the time could be discerned at night. There was no minute hand. Table clocks were not terribly reliable, though there was a good deal of sophistication in the provision of astronomical charts; the display in subsidiary dials of the positions of the moon, sun, and stars; and often the hour last struck by the chiming mechanism. The table clock went through several episodes and changes of name, particularly on the Continent where they were made in huge quantities. Sometimes they were known as tabernacle clocks, sometimes as masterpiece clocks (because an apprentice is supposed to make a masterwork to qualify). Table clocks might also feature figures and grotesques with out-of-the-way levers to point to the time, not unlike later novelty clocks.

The most important event in the history of clockmaking was the introduction of the pendulum in 1658 by Dutch physicist and astronomer Christiaan Huygens

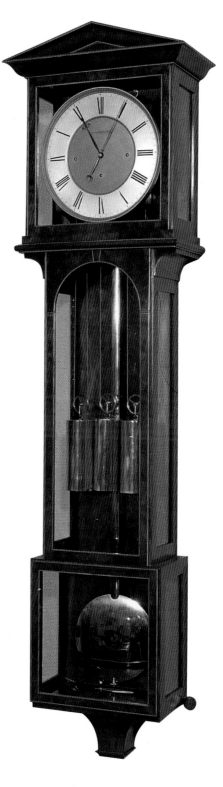

Above: A suspended pendulum wall clock with striking mechanism, three adjustable weights, and an exceptionally large bob to the pendulum. It was perhaps a regulator, a superior clock to which all the clocks of a great house or establishment were measured. The wood is fine-figured mahogany, the case superbly made, and the dial of classical simplicity.

Opposite: Dutch bracket clock by Johannes Bergeron of Amsterdam, made of ebony with silver spandrels in the unusual form of figures.

Left: A classic ebonised striking bracket clock in the architectural style by Edward East, c. 1665.

(1629–1695). This resulted in the evolution of the two most important types of clock: the bracket clock and the long-case, or grandfather, clock. Prior to the pendulum a clock was considered accurate if it lost or gained half an hour a day; the pendulum reduced the error to three minutes a week.

What might be termed the pendulum years were populated by many of the greatest English clockmakers, including the most famous of all, Thomas Tompion (1639–1713), known as "the father of English clocks." In truth he was nothing of the kind, but a fine professional who succeeded in getting himself buried in Westminster Abbey. Whether he was personally responsible for clocks bearing his name is a moot point. An immense amount of snobbery rules over classic clocks; clocks by the "names" command astronomical prices, and then there are those who somehow have not managed to get into the bible of the trade, F. J. Britten's *Old Clocks and Watches,* which lists 12,000 early makers.

Opposite: Monumental gilt German table clock of immense complexity and technical virtuosity, signed with a monogram F G S and dating from the early seventeenth century. It is set on an ebony base. Continental clocks of this quality were imported to Britain, for although British casemakers had the skill to make such timepieces, their inclination was to under-statement.

Left: A George III mahogany striking bracket clock signed Matthew Dutton of London, and an ebonised striking bracket clock with handle instead of finial by Tregent of London, both classics despite the difference in ornamentation. Both have classic gilt spandrels, and each is set on a gilt base. One clock has bun feet; the other, bracket. During this period, English clocks were unquestionably the best in the world. Some say that horology went downhill from then on.

Bracket Clocks

The bracket clock was the first truly portable clock. The name is something of a misnomer because rather than brackets it generally sports handles instead, for portability. Bracket clocks are spring-driven with a short "bob" pendulum. Because of their compactness and because clocks no longer required extraneous weights and devices, they were now regarded as decorative objects. Whereas previous types of clocks had been made predominantly of metal, they were now of wood.

In Britain, especially London, it was soon evident that bracket clocks conformed to a pattern, though the basic elements might be permutated. Clock dials were square, always of brass (enamel was rare before the 1750s), with spandrels in the corners, a "chapter ring" with the numbers in Roman numerals, a narrow outer ring with the minutes marked off in five-minute intervals, a small dial beneath the "XII" for the seconds, two winding holes sometimes covered with slide-over covers for time and strike, a date aperture, and the clockmaker's signature. Inside the case the back plate was often richly engraved—often overengraved, with a degree of elaboration that is at odds with the strict formality of the exterior.

Different nations had different approaches to clockmaking. Throughout the eighteenth century English clockmaking was supreme. In Britain the art of the clockmaker was regarded as crucial, and the cases were subsidiary. In France it was the other way around—the cabinetmaker created the surround and ordered the movements from a central workshop. By the eighteenth century it was common practice for retailers to buy movements from well-known centres such as London, Newcastle,

Above: A George II mahogany striking bracket clock with carrying handle, mahogany with classic gilt spandrels, two plain unadorned subsidiary dials, and signed by Vulliamy of London.

Right: Three French striking cartel clocks of a characteristic style, with the heavy use of buhl (or boulle), gilt, and tortoiseshell of the highest quality. They match perfectly the French furniture of the period and do not have anything at all in common with British clocks, even fairly ornate ones. Elaborate British clocks tend more towards manipulation of the wood, and buhl was never truly accepted. Sometimes French cartel or wall clocks are described by auctioneers as bracket clocks, which seems an odd thing to do, though no doubt hallowed by tradition.

and Birmingham and put their own names to them. This was easier still when white enamelled dials replaced brass, and all names on white dials are suspect, since retailers might have applied their names to blanks or whited out existing names to insert their own. With brass dials, the reverse side should be examined for unexplained screw holes or hammer marks, clues that an engraved name may have been hammered out.

Not everyone turned automatically to the bracket clock in disregard of all that had gone before. Some lantern clocks were fitted out with pendulums to keep them up to date, and a curious hybrid appeared, the hooded wall clock with old-fashioned thirty-hour rope-driven movements. Even well-known makers were involved in what were effectively dead ends, but between 1660 and 1690 there was a wave of adventure, sparked off not only by the introduction of the pendulum but by the invention of the anchor escapement in about 1670 by William Clement. Of the hundreds of escapements invented, the anchor escapement is one of the most important.

The escapement, which may be considered the small print of clockmaking, is the device that "rations" the motive power to the pendulum and provides the tick-tock. The anchor escapement is also known as the recoil escapement, in which the seconds hand of a long-case clock can be seen to shudder, or recoil, as it clicks round. The anchor escapement is so called because it looks like an anchor, pivotted centrally above the toothed wheel, slotting into the teeth as it swings backward and forward in the same plane (unlike the traditional verge escapement, which was set

Above: A pleasant average carriage clock of traditional form with little to mark it out from the ordinary run of things. The use of Arabic numerals indicates a late date, and, for some reason, are imperfectly placed, with the 2 closer to the 3 than it should be.

Right: A selection of French free-standing boudoir clocks: one gilt, one gilt and porcelain, and one of white marble with gilt decoration.

at right angles, used in some form or other since the turret clock). The anchor escapement eliminated error and made practical the use of long pendulums swinging more slowly with less cumulative error. It remained the standard escapement despite numerous attempts to improve upon it.

As clock design moved from the sober and severe, even the architectural, to the lavish, it parallelled furniture design. Although it is said that the makers of clock cases followed two decades or so behind their colleagues in cabinetmaking, the rapidity with which clocks ceased to be mere timepieces and became exquisite pieces of drawing-room furniture was phenomenal. Early bracket clocks were of ebonised oak, but since the invention of the pendulum was concurrent with the first use of walnut in furniture, it is not surprising that clock cases followed suit, as they did when mahogany was introduced in the eighteenth century. Lacquered bracket clocks were produced, but marquetry clocks are quite rare, probably because there were insufficiently large areas of wood for the cabinetmaker fully to exploit the technique.

The architectural severity of the first bracket clocks was lessened in about 1675 when the top assumed the shape of a cushion (a caddy or basket top). This persisted, with variations, for a considerable time. About 1725 cases became taller to accommodate a subsidiary dial above the main dial. Above the smaller dial was a semicircular moulding known as a break arch. The tops of the cases correspondingly increased in height, and the new shape was known as "inverted bell." The tops themselves were either of wood or of pierced and gilded brass.

The new form of bracket clock was often more aesthetically pleasing than the squarer type since the dials were more evenly spread. The earlier dials were inclined to look cluttered if there was an excess of ornament. As clockmakers became increasingly ingenious, variations abounded. Typical of the unique items was Joseph Knibb's night clock of about 1670, which incorporated an interior oil lamp necessitating a glass chimney. The time was glimpsed through a sequence of illuminated slots, necessitating an extravagantly ingenious mechanism.

There was generally little extravagance or vulgarity in bracket clocks. The variations played on them were quiet and orderly. They were in essence a transitional clock, and although occasionally used on a bracket, they were in essence little different to their nominal successors, the mantel clock.

Opposite: In 1797 William Pitt, the English prime minister, introduced an act, levying an annual tax on all clocks and watches. To help the poor, the Act of Parliament clock was devised to hang in places such as public houses where the masses disport themselves. The clock had an unglazed dial and a small trunk for a pendulum. Few were made in response to the act, but it was an attractive hanging wall clock and persisted long after the act was repealed.

Below: A fine George III striking bracket clock of mahogany and gilt, with a musical movement, the lever of which can be seen between the twin subsidiary dials, pointing towards the type of tune (including march and country dance). The musical movement was a small rotating brass cylinder with projecting pins, which, as the cylinder turned, flicked tuned prongs. As access to the constantly moving lever would be essential, the front is equipped with prominent hinges. The maker was Ellicott of London. It is a true masterpiece of the clockmaker's art from the five elaborate finials down to the exquisite Rococo-style feet.

CHAPTER TWO

ADVENT OF THE LONG-CASE

Soon after Huygens invented the pendulum in 1658, long-case clocks appeared. Freestanding, and tall enough to protect the weights and the pendulum, long-case clocks (sometimes called tall-case clocks in America) would have been an interior designer's dream, had the profession existed then. These clocks proclaimed status and acted as a focal point either in the sitting room or in the hall, at a time when the hall—rather than the living room—was becoming the first point of contact for a visitor.

There was also a psychological factor, which has received little attention. Before any means existed to perform mechanical music (the music box did not arrive for more than a hundred years), a grand house would have been a silent place, punctuated only by conversation and the chatter of servants. The steady tick-tock of a long-case clock would have provided a soothing background noise. It is not surprising that many rich enough to do so filled their houses with clocks, now regarded as an amiable eccentricity but very understandable when deathly quiet had been the norm.

The term "grandfather clock," actually considered undignified, came from a popu-

Opposite: Concept Time: an amusing evocation of time-keeping, though 'Anno 1750' is improbable, to say the least of it.

Left: Two fine mahogany long-case clocks, a mahogany hanging clock, and two barometers. The smaller long-case with the architectural pediment would perhaps be referred to as a grandmother clock, an auctioneer's term without validity. The larger clock, with its fine figuring on the wood, has two traditional globe finials with spikes, but the beading around the central panel in the trunk and on the base, together with the somewhat ungainly top, indicates that the great years of the long-case were passing. The long-case made no progress in the nineteenth century, except that towards the latter years it could become huge and contain a disc musical box, and was frequently ebonised.

Right: Prior to about 1675, long-case clocks tended towards the austere and formal, but with the advent of barley-sugar twist columns the hood was seen in a new light, and although the dial was free of decoration except spandrels, the top was often lavishly decorated. This James II walnut and marquetry clock by Edmund Appley of about 1685 has a finely carved cupid.

lar song of 1876 by Henry Clay Work. The lyrics spoke of "my grandfather's clock," which "stopped dead, never to go again." The song referred to the clock as "too tall for the shelf" and listeners rashly assumed that the lyricist was writing about a long-case clock. How potent is the power of popular song! The miniature long-case was naturally known as a grandmother clock, though it was more likely to have been a "regulator," a superior long-case to which all the other clocks in the house were regulated.

Although long-case and bracket clocks rendered obsolete all preceding clocks by reason of their sophistication and the use of the latest technology, older-type clocks were still used. Some were converted, as clocks continued to be upgraded, or sometimes "downgraded," when old elements (such as the verge escapement) that had been replaced were later put back by dedicated clock enthusiasts in the interests of historical accuracy.

The hooded wall clock with hanging weights was still being made, sometimes

Left: A magnificent clock of about 1673 with walnut oyster veneer, barley-sugar twist columns, and a flat top. It has perfect proportions and simple restrained gilt metal adornments. The clockmaker is Edward East.

Below: During the nineteenth century there were increasing trade links between Japan and China and the western world, and although the influence of Japan on Britain was far more significant than the other way around, the concept of the free-standing clock clearly had an influence on the Japanese, to a somewhat bizarre effect, as this black lacquered clock of about 1840 shows.

Opposite: The French did not have the long-case clock; their standing clock was known as a pedestal clock, and it never achieved the classic status of their mantel and cartel clocks. Rich in gilding, this handsome and prestigious ebony clock has an expanded finial far more extravagant than those on English clocks. It belongs to the Louis XVI period (1754–1793), and the clockmaker was Ferdinant Berthoud of Paris.

Left: The black japanned (lacquered) long-case clock enjoyed a vogue long after the method had been rejected by furniture makers, but was far more common on long-case clocks than on table, wall or mantel clocks. It is rare to find a japanned clock in anything like perfect condition, as the gold decoration on the black lacquer has usually faded or flaked off. In Japan, many coats of lacquer would have been painstakingly applied. This was not often the case in Britain, where the case maker was inferior in status to the clockmaker who provided the movement.

with the fashionable new marquetry. The neat and functional movements of both long-case and bracket clocks did not stop the continued production of turret clocks, those sprawling monsters of iron (often with wooden components) for churches and public buildings, though new developments such as the anchor escapement were incorporated instead of the verge escapement. As late as 1735 a timber-framed turret clock was made for the church of Barton-in-Fabis in Nottinghamshire, looking very much like an old-fashioned wooden mangle, with most of the wheelwork of iron. However, since turret clocks were made to be hidden away, there was no demand for improved appearance.

Above: The hood of a Regency long-case clock by Grove of London, impressive but lacking in refinement. The traditional layout of the dial with chapter rings and gilt spandrels in the corners was replaced by painting, often of a perfunctory kind.

Long - Case Design

The long-case clock developed at the same time as the bracket clock, and shared characteristics, in particular the layout of the dial. The first long-case clocks had verge escapements of the old style and short pendulums; only with the introduction of the anchor escapement was the longer pendulum introduced.

The long-case clock features three divisions: the hood, the trunk, and the plinth. The bottom of the plinth was often flush with the floor, but many are fitted with bun feet, perhaps for a practical reason. In an age when floors were by no means

Opposite: The maker of this clock, James Harrison (1704–1766), is not to be confused with John Harrison, the inventor of the marine chronometer. This ebony long-case clock of 1728 has many unusual features, with tasteful gilt work and a 'bulls-eye' window so that the swing of the pendulum could be seen. In the later all-mahogany long-cases, this device was little used.

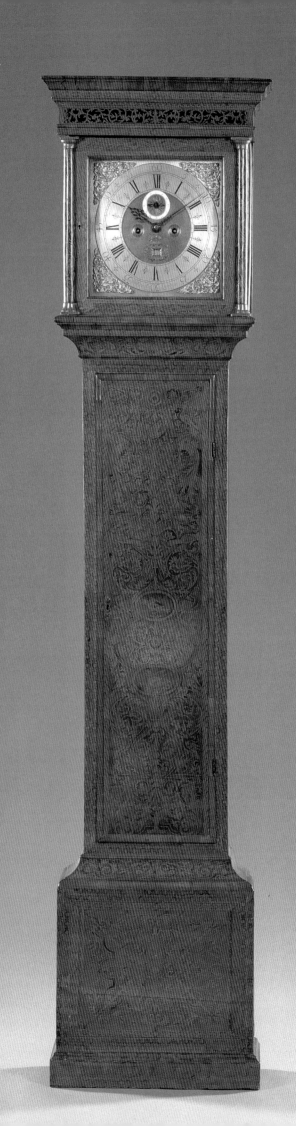

Opposite: The best of clockmakers preferred a quiet grain; the earliest of long-case clockmakers used ebonised wood without decoration. This fine clock has a busy veneer, perhaps not to the taste of all.

Left: It might be speculated that Regency long-case clocks are more popular than the less ornate clocks of the eighteenth century because they are more spectacular. However, there was a price to pay. The hood grew out of proportion, and as it became much larger than the plinth, the clock could appear top-heavy. This happened, too, in eighteenth-century clocks. The additional half arch above the dial could be overloaded, in this case with additional spandrels, and subsidiary dials were often placed awkwardly. The ornamental cartouche on the trunk is not reflected elsewhere and seems to have been added to fill an empty space.

regular, it was simpler to ensure that the clock sat absolutely vertical by shaving off part of a bun foot, rather than having to saw off a section of plinth. Plinths were often altered, sometimes to give a clock added height. Early long-case clocks were slim and not extremely tall (six feet, six inches, on average), but they got taller and wider, both for reasons of prestige and to accommodate longer pendulums with a wider swing. (It is erroneously believed that the pendulum invariably beats the second; the thirty-nine inch "Royal" pendulum does beat a second, but the five-foot pendulum has a one-and-a-quarter-second swing.)

As with bracket clocks, early cases before about 1675 had an architectural character, formal and austere with ebonised wood much in evidence. Detail on the hood was at first confined to columns, either straight or with spiral turning known as barley-sugar twist. This simplicity did not last long once cabinetmakers saw the

Above: A handsome, refined hanging mahogany wall clock with glass over the pendulum and a separate panel over the large pendulum bob. Despite the architectural pediment associated with early long-case clocks, this is much later, as is evident from the plain dial with the gilded surround.

Right: Lacquer had been used by the Chinese as early as the fourth century B.C., but it was only in the sixteenth and seventeenth centuries that large pieces in lacquer were exported to the west. It was widely copied, the composition of the lacquer often changed by the addition of shellac. Western case makers of long-case clocks assimilated the Japanese style with amazing skill, as seen in this Queen Anne clock by William Scafe of London. As lacquering went into decline, standards fell until it became no more than varnishing. The French developed lacquering into a high art; it is known as vernis Martin, after the Martin brothers who evolved it. Even further from oriental lacquer was the Italian lacca contrafatta.

Left: This eighteenth-century lacquered long-case clock by Samuel Short must be one of the most slender ever made, but it is quite short so that it is not overpowering. At a time when cases were being widened to give long pendulums more room to swing and thus increase accuracy, this charming clock went against the trends. Whereas many hoods look too large for the base, the reverse is the case here. The decoration on the lacquer is multi-coloured, which was not common.

Above: A French mantel clock of strongly veined marble and ormolu, with accompanying candlesticks to form a garniture (a clock set). The French excelled in such pieces, often taking their invention into the realm of fantasy, but this clock is superb, with the quantity of ormolu as against marble nicely balanced.

potential of long-case clocks as a showpiece for their work. Clock case design reflected all the great advances in furniture stemming from the increasing use of walnut and the arrival of Continental ideas in Britain—marquetry, lacquer, and walnut veneer, as well as elements taken from French furniture such as the use of *boulle* (brass and tortoiseshell). There were some extravaganzas, such as the long-case clock japanned in ivory—the rarest and most desirable colour—made by the great clockmaker Daniel Quare about 1710.

Decoration could be applied to the trunk in almost any form, usually mirrored in the plinth. Marquetry and parquetry designs were sometimes set in oval or round panels against a plain background, sometimes of oystershell veneering (in which the veneer comes from thin slices of branches) in olive wood or laburnum. The edges of the door fronting the pendulum were often adorned with cock beading, a half-round moulding that hid the gap between the sides of the door and the trunk.

To display the movement of the pendulum, the centre of the trunk might possess a round or oval window, either of plain glass or of distorting "bull's-eye" glass. Many

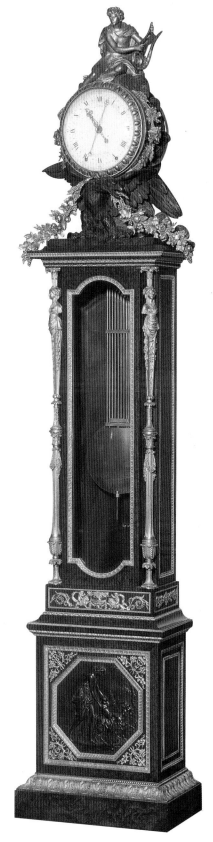

clockmakers disdained this feature because it broke up the surface of the trunk and any veneer work presented an added complication.

Although the marquetry and veneer on clock cases could be powerful it is said that Thomas Tompion himself always preferred the simplicity of undecorated ebonised cases even into the eighteenth century, although he too was subject to the market. His designs are very masculine and unfussy in character, though he was obliged to top his hoods with finials and added extras. The ball-and-spire finials were perhaps the most excessive, and it became common practice to build up the hood until was almost overpowering, and often out of proportion with the rest of the clock.

Over the years many of the hoods have disappeared. There is no great mystery to this. As long-case clocks ceased to be the preserve of the rich they found their way into farmhouses and other homes with lower ceilings. Since the upper part of the hood served no purpose other than decoration, it was often unceremoniously removed so the now flat-topped clock could be accommodated.

Historical progression enables clocks to be dated by the size of the dials and the style of the numerals. Until 1690 dials measured ten inches; from 1690 to 1700 they reached eleven inches, with twelve inches to the arched dial. From about 1660 to 1665 numerals were small; from 1665 to about 1690 numerals to indicate date were added; from about 1685 to 1695 a seconds ring was added; and from about 1695 to 1720 a larger minute ring was provided.

Added Features and Extravaganzas

As the movements of long-case clocks were approaching perfection—or as near to perfection as mattered—there was a constant interest in providing something other than the correct time. The opportunity arose around 1720 with the use of the

Previous page, left: A quaint Victorian marble clock, showing how the refinement of the eighteenth century was giving way to absurdities. Black marble (or slate) and inlay is coupled with gilt fittings of a strange kind, with a meaningless finial and carrying handles, the purpose of which is unclear. The dial, made by the clockmaker and not the casemaker, is refreshingly sober. During this period, the manufacture of a clock was distributed amongst various types of workers, and this may account for the lack of a coherent design.

Previous page, right: When intended for the Court, price was no object. This incredible Louis XVI clock with barometers was one of a pair made for Marie Antoinette, the case by Weisweiler and Beneman, the clock movement by Robin, and the barometer movement by Mossy. It is fitted with a bar pendulum, more favoured in France than Britain. The quality of the ormolu fittings is staggering, incorporating caryatids (female figures used as supporting columns), and the figure with a lyre at the top of a quality that would be impossible to surpass. Had the French Revolution not destroyed the culture that fostered such art objects, one wonders what the future of European applied art would have been.

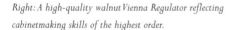

Right: A high-quality walnut Vienna Regulator reflecting cabinetmaking skills of the highest order.

arched dial, in which a semicircular brass plate was fitted above the square dial. Initially this provided space for another subsidiary dial, but makers speedily realised that by using the motive power of the clock movement, the semicircular space could sport such novelties as a display of the transition of the stars or the procession of the moon.

The first arched dials of 1720 were followed by the arched moon dials ten years later. Although the solemn procession of the moon was modestly interesting, the presence of a large open space above the dial provided the opportunity for theatrics. The moon was replaced by ships, figures, almost anything that struck the fancy of the clockmaker. With a little rejigging of the movement, objects could be made to move up and down or side to side or engage in almost any permutation of actions. This trend was even more popular among European clockmakers. The painter Zoffany, later a distinguished portraitist, was said to have started off by painting on clocks.

The roominess inside the clock case provided ample space for extras, including

automata, musical movements, and sounding and chiming mechanisms, all of which could be very elaborate. A clock by Andrews of Bristol of 1810 had thirty-two bells and sixty-four hammers; each successive day it played a different tune, accompanied by miniature musicians and dancers in the arch. On Sunday the shutters came down and a stern message appeared: "Remember the Lord's Day and Keep it Holy!" Extravaganzas reached their zenith in the late nineteenth century, when monster clocks more than ten feet tall were fitted out with disc musical movements, often with penny-in-the-slot mechanisms for use in public houses and other places of entertainment.

Added extras could be quite tasteful, or they might be quaint or grotesquely amateurish even if the rest of the clock was of fine quality. Quality was helped by self-applied restrictions on the use of dial ornament. The corner spandrels, sometimes just ornamental and sometimes depicting cupids, could be finely done or be crude castings, but they preserved a certain decorum; poor quality is evident only upon close examination.

Right: John Harrison was one of the great names in clockmaking, and his marine chronometer of 1772 revolutionised navigation, enabling the master of a ship to find out exactly where he was at sea. This is a reproduction of Harrison's No 1 timekeeper made by Sinclair Harding of Cheltenham, skeletonised so that all the parts can be seen working. The skeleton clock enjoyed wide popularity in the nineteenth century, and when one comes up at auction there is a keen demand.

Opposite: Three eighteenth-century long-case clocks, one a miniature, with broken pediments. The white enamel dial had arrived, and with it the practise of painting them. The quality of the painting was rarely as good as the quality of the metal spandrels. The clock on the right has a half-arch on which is represented the phases of the moon. The miniature has a half-arch representing the sea, which no doubt goes up and down to amuse the spectator. Bad taste was creeping in, even during these George III years. The gilt fittings on the pediment of the clock on the right detract from the design, and the mottled effect on the upper part of the hood would have made the furniture makers shudder. Flame mahogany veneer is applied incompletely, so there is no 'mirror' effect as in the best quartering (placing identical veneers side by side).

Clockmakers were subject to the laws of supply and demand, and if they could promote themselves beyond signing their work they would be happy to do so. Any royal or aristocratic and scientific appointments were exploited to the full. It is impossible to say what clockmakers thought of the developments in their field, and whether they realised that the golden age of the long-case clock was passing after hardly more than half a century. In a sense they were caught up in the more rapid pace of history, dedicated craftsmen of an age that was already seeing the first crackling signs of the Industrial Revolution and the increasing quest for novelty. They were in competition with the makers of novelty clocks, such as the astronomical musical clock with automata ten feet high designed in the grand Baroque style by Henry Bridges (c. 1697–1754), who betrayed an almost medieval desire for mechanical complexity. Although this piece and a similar creation by Jacob Lovelace of Exeter (1656–1716) are no longer in existence, fragments survive to show that they were not mere speculations but viable timepieces with an inordinate amount of added extras.

George Graham and John Harrison

Perhaps this assessment is too pessimistic. As clockmakers—rather than as purveyors of eye-catching visual effects—the British led the field. The most gifted, not excluding Tompion, was George Graham (1673–1751), one of the great names in science and not just clockmaking. Apprenticed to the clockmaker Henry Aske in London in 1688, Graham entered the service of Tompion in 1695, later marrying Tompion's niece. Over the course of his career, Graham made about 3,000 watches

Above: A Regency clock set, the clock with an applied swag decoration. The clock and accompanying sidepieces are topped by what appear to be trays, the reason for which is difficult to see. With the decline of the bracket clock British clockmakers were at a loss to come up with a replacement, and although many talented clockmakers took their lead from the ornate French mantel clock, traditionalists were wary, and probably reluctant to borrow ideas from a nation still viewed as the time-honoured enemy.

Previous pages: In the UK, the term 'chronometer' applies to a timepiece specifically designed for maritime use to find the longitude. Although these three chronometers are modern— the first by George Edward Frodsham dating from about 1865, the second by Carl Ranch of about 1907, and the third an American chronometer—they differ little from the early chronometers of the late eighteenth century. The brass inserts on the edges of each case are not ornamental, but are intended to give added protection to the box itself; this device was also used in military campaign furniture such as chests.

and 174 clocks, was elected to the Royal Society, and in about 1709 made the first orrery, a clockwork-driven scientific instrument illustrating the movements of the planets round the sun.

After Tompion died in 1713, Graham invented the deadbeat escapement, a type of anchor escapement with no recoil. The deadbeat remained the standard type for most precision clocks until the advent of the electric clock. The teeth of the toothed wheel were very fine with sharp points, so the pallet surfaces (the ends of the arms of the anchor) were often jewelled with sapphire or garnet to prevent wear. Made with greater precision than the anchor, the deadbeat was usually set up in association with the mercurial pendulum of 1721, which compensated the pendulum for changes of temperature.

Perhaps only the accomplishments of John Harrison (1693–1776) are of the calibre of Graham's. A carpenter by trade, Harrison spent nearly a lifetime of work in quest of an accurate timepiece, in response to an open challenge issued by the British government for a method to measure longitude accurately, which was impossible without accurate timing. Harrison developed his own escapement, the grasshopper. His ultimate invention, the chronometer—which looked something like an alarm clock and measured just over five inches in diameter—eventually won him £20,000 (well over £1 million in today's money) from the Board of Longitude. In trials at sea in 1761 Harrison's chronometer gained only fifty-four seconds in five months.

The Decline of the Long-Case

The middle of the eighteenth century saw the relative decline of the London clock trade and the emergence of the provincial maker. Country makers had largely escaped the novelty-seeking of the London market. Their work, though perhaps old-fashioned, was more restrained and classical, with less escape into affectation and whimsy. Imagination was still in evidence, however, with dots substituted for minute lines, and the maker's name sometimes appearing around the half-dial. As in furniture, the swan's-neck pediment became a feature of good clocks, and columns descending from the hood were often freestanding.

Since country makers usually never got as far as London they had to rely on their own sense of aesthetics about proportions; hence country clocks often have an oddity of scale, as though slightly squashed. Even more than were the London makers, country makers were dependent on their customers, who formed a narrow social spectrum. Squires and yeoman farmers and a sprinkling of professionals such as surgeons would have had an inkling of what was fashionable in London, and expected their clockmakers to provide something similar.

Clockmaking in London was mainly a question of tinkering with externals. The calendar dial instead of a date aperture came into vogue in the 1770s, and seconds circles were engraved, not pinned on as previously. The various styles through which furniture evolved were passed on to the clock case makers, but as furniture was inclined to be trimmed down, clocks were increasingly piled with excrescences. This was especially true with the Chippendale–Gothic mood, impressive but ill at ease with the most urbane and polite furniture in Europe. Neoclassicism was not suited to long-case clocks, and the motifs implanted on them looked absurd.

With the painted dial, there came a fashion for mottoes such as "Time is Valuable" and "The Man Is Yet Unborn that Duly Weighs an Hour," a particular fad of makers and purchasers in northern England. The painted dial had its supporters; it was much easier to read. It also had its detractors; there was far too much empty space for an overexuberant clock artist to decorate, resulting in much ghastly output. Painted dials was an industry; in Birmingham alone there were forty firms providing made-to-order dials with a specified name and place, and perhaps laudable maxims as well, in or out of Brummagem dialect.

The gloriously muddled styles of Victorian furniture were repeated in long-case clocks, often cheaply produced, with machine-cut elements, gluing, and low-quality movements set in grandiloquent creations. Many of the long-cases in Victorian homes were hand-me-downs, and there was no great enthusiasm for creating them; they were out of date. Fortunately, long-case clocks have an amazing survival ability, simply because the technology is so good and the wheelwork resists rust.

The Arts and Crafts movement produced some delightful stained oak long-case clocks. Although desperate attempts were later made at modernist clocks, they were never less than laughable.

The long-case clock was the logical product of the long pendulum. The long pendulum fell out of fashion, and so did the clock. That it lasted as long as it did, creeping into the nineteenth century, is remarkable. In the 1930s a modest long-case was a suburban status symbol, though hardly more than the oak mantel clock with Westminster chimes. Some of these "long-case" clocks did not even have a long pendulum; the door opened to reveal a cocktail cabinet.

Above: Mainland European clockmakers did not produce an over-abundance of long-cases, preferring instead to concentrate on mantel clocks such as this dignified German example from the late nineteenth century.

CHAPTER THREE

MANTEL AND WALL CLOCKS

T he Continent had not been heavily involved in the long-case clock, though there are fine examples from Holland and elsewhere. There was a close connection between Dutch and English clockmakers; the Dutch made their own superb cases to fit the superior English movements. Some Continental clocks have no parallel in England, such as the extravagant bombé (swelled out) Dutch and French clocks, or the painted pine Swedish clocks. European clocks often featured arched hoods. The bulk of European long-case clocks lack the gravitas and confidence of English clocks; clearly it was not a clockmaking form that greatly appealed to Europeans. But this was not the case with the mantel clock.

The French Influence

The mantel clock greatly resembled the bracket clock except that there were no carrying handles. The invention of the mantelpiece provided a logical resting place for a clock, as well as the best focal point in a sitting room. There was therefore no limit to what could be done with a mantel clock; it was a form of applied art and

Opposite: A George III musical bracket clock in tortoiseshell and ormolu by Benjamin Barber of London. In clocks as well as in furniture, types of specific items are inclined to be increasingly elaborate and ornate; this is often unfortunate. But not with the bracket clock, and this marvellous clock is one of the great masterpieces of the genre, rich yet not gaudy. An individual feature is the replacement of the numbers on the dial with abstract shapes—very innovative for the period.

Below: A French garniture in white marble and ormolu, with a sunburst-motif pendulum, and the whole surmounted by an eagle with outspread wings. These clocks are difficult to date as they were made throughout the nineteenth century without much loss of quality.

Opposite: A Louis XV clock with ormolu, porcelain flowers, and metal Chinese figures by the Vincennes porcelain factory, The creator of the surround was Jacques-Jerome Gudin, who died in 1789. The movement by James Grohe is of later date. The glory of the French mantel clock was the casework, and the movement, often spring-driven, was slotted in later. The soft-paste Vincennes factory moved to Sevres in 1765, and made porcelain in the style of the Paris factories until 1788.

Below: An elaborate spring-driven French marble and ormolu clock, accompanied by a selection of Wedgwood pottery. The French called the mantel clock the pendule de chiminée; the term pendule applies to freestanding clocks, whether intended for the mantelpiece or not.

science in which there were no rules, not even the necessity of a dial.

A mantel clock could be severely functional, it could be meaninglessly ornate, it could be witty and clever, and it could engross the attention of artists, cabinetmakers, workers in precious metals and brass, sculptors, enamellers, potters, and even clockmakers themselves. The movements might be good, bad, or indifferent, but with the relative precision of the most ordinary clock technology and a studied indifference to accuracy—one of the characteristics of the clock-buying class—it did not matter terribly much.

Although the term *mantel clock* is English, its most spectacular manifestations were in France, owing not so much to greater ingenuity or the taste of the upper classes—which was becoming international—but to the patronage of the French court. The *Horologers du Roi* were privileged clock- and watchmakers who worked under the protection of the king. Under Louis XIV, the Sun King, the laws of supply and demand that dominated the British clock industry were irrelevant. Art objects were created regardless of expense, and outrageous experiments could be made knowing it would not reflect badly on a balance sheet.

Many of the case-making processes were delicate and there was bound to be a good deal of wastage. The earliest examples of the French mantel clock were the *religieuses*. Though architectural and quite formal, they displayed the evident delight in expensive methods of decoration, as in the use of tortoiseshell veneer and silver and brass inlay. Characteristic of French clocks was the method of displaying the numerals, each on its own individual enamel plaque or cartouche. The number itself was enamelled in black, and sometimes in blue at a later date. It might be said

that the requisite for a French clock—especially of the 1730s and after—was that all blank spaces must be decorated. (The main exception is in the fine French long-case regulator clocks, which are as austere as the best English examples.)

The French developed their own escapements, and a particular feature of their pendulums is that they follow a gridiron pattern, comprising up to nine rods of alternate brass and steel to effect temperature compensation. Whether this was more efficient than George Graham's mercurial pendulum is uncertain, but the rejection of this and the decision to ignore Graham's deadbeat escapement is difficult to understand when it was widely accepted that British clockmaking was the best in Europe. It can only be supposed that it was deemed unimportant; certainly the French kings would not have been interested in absolute accuracy, and the same would have been true of anybody but astronomers and seafarers. Had there been a need to compete in the marketplace the path of French clockmaking would unquestionably have taken a different direction—and the world would have been the poorer without these extravagant luxuries, impossible to forge or even meddle with, evidence of what could be made in a country of consummate craftsmen when money was no object.

At times it seems that the artists involved in the creation of surrounds (they can hardly be called cases) invented problems just for the delight of solving them, as in

Above: Dial and gilt surround of an elaborate French clock, though not of the highest quality, as the work is routine and tired.

Right: A collection of bracket clocks of various periods in mahogany and ebonised wood. The miniatures, which are rather restrained in appearance, can hardly be called bracket clocks, and the carrying handle of the clock on the extreme right suggests a different type of clock altogether. The plain miniature bears the well-known name of Vulliamy of London, and may well have been intended as a travelling clock. The George III clocks are of high quality, with the ebonised clock equipped with a calendar aperture.

applying inlay of tortoiseshell, pewter, brass, stained horn, and seashell on undulating surfaces. In the same way French cabinetmakers made chests *(commodes)* on which exposed surfaces required veneer even though the surfaces went in several directions at once—bulging, concave, convex, and serpentine.

Although the French were not partial to the long-case clock, they had an equivalent—the pedestal clock, an elaborate timepiece set on a highly decorated stand, ornamented with gilded mounts and impossibly intricate marquetry in which the great French furniture guilds, the *ébénistes,* played their part. Until the Régence (1715–23) there had been a degree of formality, but with the arrival of the Rococo style (a prettification of Baroque) there came a preoccupation with flowing curved lines, a degree of asymmetry, and a new formal device. The centre of the dial became an enamel plaque, and it evolved into such an established feature that the layout came to be known as the thirteen-piece dial.

The shape of clocks became so convoluted that they no longer had a base, and many were now wall-mounted or cartel clocks, where the dial peeped out from a mass of flowers, foliage, cherubs, suns, classical motifs, or almost anything else. Any material could be used. Sometimes bronze was deliberately given a patina (usually associated with the natural ageing process) in an attempt to produce something new. On one of the most charming of such items the clock, a white-dial plain affair, is set above a bank of bookshelves, while the foreground features a lady seated at a writing table, meticulously sculpted in bronze. In a popular theme, a clock was sometimes set against a lyre, an antique musical instrument akin to the Irish harp. a novelty clock that itself swung from a gridiron pendulum above.

Opposite: Louis XV ormolu and porcelain mantel clock made in Paris with the porcelain from Meissen, still the most important porcelain factory in Europe. Although hard-paste porcelain had only been invented quite recently, the workmanship is stunning. The subject is typical of the time; it reflected a bucolic world of shepherdesses and shepherds, harlequins and strumming musicians far away from real life.

Left: French nineteenth-century marble and ormolu clock in the form of a tower, with the surface of the marble intersected with fine lines to suggest brickwork. The case bears an animal mask for no other reason than to break up a plain surface. It is difficult to think of a more unpromising subject for a timepiece.

Overleaf, top: French nineteenth-century garniture comprising onyx and ormolu clock with pillars and vases, and reflecting a passing interest in Greek architecture.

Overleaf, below: Two-coloured marble clock in the Greek style with gilt presented in a pattern of dots or lines, a type of decoration that was to prove common throughout the nineteenth century in Europe, Britain, and the United States. It became an obsessive device, as though the makers disliked the appearance of any plain surface.

Opposite: A classic Charles II ebonised bracket clock of the late seventeenth century, complete with carrying handle, a feature which was inclined to be dropped as the caddy became more ornate. Ebonised furniture has never been fully accepted by those in the antique trade, who regard it is as somehow inferior, without reason. Ebonising was not a way of disguising cheap wood, as is often thought.

Cartel clocks were sometimes made of carved wood, coated with gesso (plaster of Paris and size), and gilded. English versions were made to complement Chippendale-style furnishings. Ceramics were rarely used in English clocks before the nineteenth century, but quite often porcelain of the highest quality—Meissen and Sèvres—was incorporated in French timepieces, usually in combination with other materials. With the approach of Neoclassicism, Egyptian, Roman, and Greek motifs were extensively used, as were animal and human forms, and sometimes entire rooms were provided as a setting for the clock.

This exuberance was cut dramatically short by the French Revolution, and in the nineteenth century the French had to compete on equal terms with the English, the Germans, the Swiss, and increasingly the Americans, as they were obliged to do in the other applied arts such as furniture and ceramics.

The Development of the Wall Clock

There are several kinds of wall clocks: public service clocks, and clocks for the house, either lavish cartels or more humdrum efforts retailing for little money. Public service clocks are large, fixed to the wall or suspended from or fixed on beams (the railway station clock). Diversions like subsidiary dials are uncommon because the main object is for the clocks to be read at a distance. They must also be reliable, far more reliable than the traditional public service clock—the church or municipal building clock.

A 1797 tax on clocks and watches caused such outrage that it was speedily repealed, since it meant hardship not only for the public but for the clockmakers as

Opposite: Staggering bracket clock by Eardley Norton, with ormolu, tortoiseshell, untreated metal for the serpents flanking the finial, and—rare for an English clock—the imbedding of gems though purists deplore the arrival of the white enamel dial, here it is essential to give contrast to the opulence.

Above: Of equal magnificence is this clock by Godin of Paris, with porcelain Chinoiserie figures. Unlike most Chinoiserie figures, these characters are given a firm individuality, as they would have been had the piece been crafted in China or Japan. Perhaps the most spectacular aspect of this porcelain and ormolu clock is the checkerboard pattern on the cloak of the figure on the left.

Above: A selection of nineteenth-century skeleton clocks. The Gothic style, as in the third from the left, was the most often used. Much ingenuity was used to fashion new types of dials, and sometimes these became so convoluted that it is difficult to discern the numerals, on the clock on the right.

Opposite: On the left is an early nineteenth-century rosewood clock barometer with mother-of-pearl inlay by Calderara of London. The clock is of less importance than the barometer. Many barometers, such as the Admiral Fitzroy version, had nautical descriptions of the weather; but this one bears the sequence: change, fair, set fair, very dry, stormy, much rain, and rain. The barometer on the right is French, of a similar period, and made by Leydecker.

well. Yet it indicated that there was a great demand for public clocks in places where people congregated, such as public houses. Once clocks were established it was soon clear that they were appreciated and they remained a constant feature. Dial clocks were either completely circular or they had a compartment beneath (called a "salt box"); they were basic verge-escapement clocks with short pendulums.

Tavern clocks of the 1720s onward are often erroneously called Act of Parliament clocks. With their long pendulums they resembled lower-end long-case clocks without their settled formalistic devices such as corner spandrels. The first spring-driven clocks with short pendulums date from about 1750. About 1770 the trunk assumed a rounded form, known as the teardrop, and this coexisted for a time with the square abbreviated trunk, which in itself was cut down. The completely round dial lasted until almost the present day.

The round-dial clock was the clockmaker's bread and butter in the nineteenth century, for with the coming of the railway, clocks had to be synchronised to accord with railway timetables. They thus had to be reliable. By 1896 there were 21,277 miles of railway line in Great Britain and hundreds of stations, some of which had several clocks, which were often double-sided. Almost all the thousands of official and municipal buildings had large clocks, as did shops, where the clocks extended over the pavement at right angles. Almost all were white-dial clocks, usually painted plate zinc.

Perhaps the most celebrated wall clock—as opposed to the most common—was the Vienna regulator, heavily carved and extremely handsome. The Americans favoured the banjo clock, invented in 1802 by Simon Willard (1753–1848). This type incorporated scenes into the design of the clock; Mount Vernon and the victory of Perry over the British at Lake Erie during the 1812 war were especially popu-

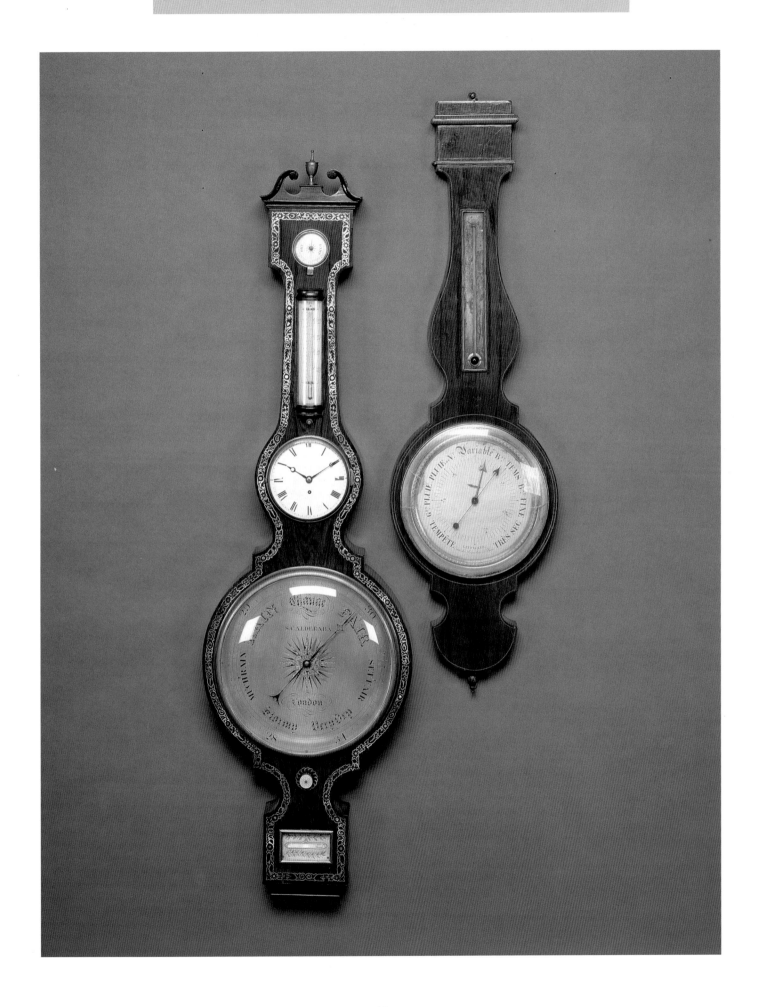

Above: A pair of Victorian black marble clocks, one with an attractive inlay of pictorial motifs and greatly superior to the general run of marble (often actually slate) clocks.

Opposite: A French Rococo clock with a porcelain case by Meissen, a well-modelled nude figure at the top of the clock, and an unsigned movement. The Rococo movement, a prettified version of the more austere baroque, reappeared at intervals, usually as a reaction against straight lines and formality.

lar. French clocks had an influence in Britain; some examples indicate that had circumstances been propitious, England might have followed the same path of conspicuous consumption—if someone had footed the bill. And none of the Georges was prepared to do this. There was a tradition for English astronomical and scientific clocks, typical of which was a fine rotating globe above a movement made by John Whitehurst (1713–1788), a member of the celebrated Lunar Society of Birmingham.

A fellow Lunar Society member, the industrialist Matthew Boulton, made the gilded brass case. Boulton was involved with superior English mantel clocks, making clock cases mounted with Blue John stone from Derbyshire (a type of native marble). Josiah Wedgwood also provided blue-and-white jasper plaques for high-quality mantel clocks, but the bracket clock remained the standard English clock with relatively few alterations.

The nineteenth century saw a mixture of styles. Where money was involved and taste was no object, the English mantel clock became either an object of awe or one of desperation. As in France, mantel clocks were increasingly flanked by side ornaments, making a garniture. Sometimes these odd creations—neither vases nor anything conceivably useful, and often made of cheap materials such as zinc—are seen languishing in antique shops.

Above: An elegant early-nineteenth century marble clock with ormolu feet, carrying handles, gilt stringing, and a gilt figure.

Right: The bracket clock was the quintessential English clock. Regency clockmakers came up with this elegant variant (left) in rosewood with urn finial, gilt plinth, tiny bun feet, stream-lined shape, and bombé sidepieces. It has a sweep calender hand, but as the numbers only come to thirty it would have to be manually adjusted during longer or shorter months. The small pedimented satinwood clock might be described as a boudoir clock, charming and unpretentious, and the clock on the right by Brockbanks and Atkins of London is a rather unusual medley of styles.

One of the few distinguished clocks of the period was the balloon clock, datable to about 1800, with a narrow waist and usually with an inlaid motif beneath the dial. They were usually of mahogany with satinwood inlay. Bracket clocks continued to be made, often with a Gothic gloss—pointed arches, extravagant finials, more rectangular—though more bizarre Gothic clocks were made for the Great Exhibition of 1851. The same exhibition displayed clocks of Parian (porcelain imitating marble) and electroplated metal. Doulton produced multicolour pottery cases; with the increased emphasis on mass production, however, the movements were imported, usually from Germany, though occasionally from France, which had had much experience with novelty clocks and associated compact movements.

Roman numerals had been dropped on some painted dials of the eighteenth century, and Arabic numerals were now much used. Clock movements were now made in factories and not workshops, and the clockmaker was hardly more than an artisan. Parts were stamped out and assembled by semiskilled operatives. There was the widest of gaps between the mass producers and the elite. The Dent clock made for Greenwich Observatory in 1872 was the most accurate all-mechanical clock ever made, with an error of one-hundredth of a second a day.

The archetypal Victorian mantel clock is in the form of a Greek temple with pillars, often in a garniture. It is customarily "black marble," which is actually slate. Produced in immense quantities, they were cheap because of the competition from abroad. In the 1960s such clocks were bought in junk shops and street markets for five shillings (25p); they were then thrown on the pavement and smashed so the

Opposite: The poor man's Meissen, a run-of-the-mill movement inserted into a pottery case. The decoration is above average for this type of mass-produced clock, and the shape of the case is orthodox Rococo and by no means ugly. This kind of clock is more rare than one would imagine.

Below: The most common type of Victorian black marble / slate mantel clock, made in the form of a Greek temple. This one is rather superior to most as there is a contrasting design beneath the sloping pediment.

Above: Victorian marble clock with gilt birds and the black marble alleviated by panels of variegated marble. The fashion for black marble is difficult to understand; sometimes wooden clocks were lacquered black to simulate genuine marble. These were considerably cheaper.

drumlike movement could be retrieved. They were surprisingly good movements, as were the movements of preelectric car clocks, which were extracted from old or crashed cars and fitted into a more appropriate case.

The skeleton clock—originating in France in the late eighteenth century but made on quite a large scale in Britain—featured a stripped-down clock movement of architectural type mounted on a wooden plinth and displayed under a glass dome. Gothic skeleton clocks, sold by catalogue from a firm in Clerkenwell, London, were working clocks but were presented as curios; the dial was often too difficult or swamped with irrelevant detail to read. Skeleton clocks are still much in demand today, and many "clock men" have found making them to be a profitable hobby.

German and American Clocks

Prestige clockmaking of the last half of the nineteenth century was unquestionably tired. There seemed no advances to make; even if there were there would be no financial incentive. The greatest enterprise was in Germany and America. The Black Forest had a tradition of do-it-yourself clocks from the late seventeenth century. *Everything* was made of wood, including the whole of the movement, and the weights were stones from the nearest stream. The farmers who made these for themselves turned clockmakers. Although the pendulum had been invented in 1657, Black Forest clockmakers did not use it until 1740, and then placed the pendulum in front of the dial.

The first Black Forest clocks needed winding every twelve hours, and lost or gained about twenty minutes a day. Striking mechanisms appeared in 1730 about the same time as the cuckoo—the most famous clock in the world, which reached

Left: A steeple-shaped shelf clock of the nineteenth century made by Jerome and Company of New Haven, a pioneer of mass production. This is a superior early example. Chauncey Jerome (1793–1860) began business in about 1821, and in 1855 the company was renamed the New Haven Clock Company. Jerome published A History of the American Clock Business in 1860.

its quintessential form in 1870. Early dials were of wood, then of paper, pasted onto the wood; the next step, unusual in clockmaking, was to raise the circular part of the dial from the background. Production became specialised: one person made the movement, another did the carving, and in some Alpine eyrie someone else made cuckoos. Brass wheels replaced those of wood, and brass bells replaced those of glass.

In terms of international impact, the American clocks were more important, even though the German clocks were retailing at only fifteen shillings (75p). The make-your-own-clock industry started in 1807. Clocks were supplied in kit form, sent from the United States by mail order. The concept was unlike any clock that had come before. Known as shelf clocks, they contained forty parts, which could be assembled in a matter of minutes. The back of the rectangular case contained advertising material and instructions, and a picture could be stuck onto the bottom half of the glass. Veneer was used instead of staining making the finish better than that on German clocks. They came in various styles: the Ogee; the Round Gothic, called the Beehive; and the Sharp Gothic, the favourite, which was made in millions and was a treasured design for alarm clocks into the 1940s.

Disdainful, the British did not enter the competition, but they were sufficiently alarmed to impose taxes on imported American clocks. Realizing the threat to their market, the Germans produced the picture clock around 1840. This contained a smallish movement in the centre of an ornately framed picture, but the weights drooping below the frame spoiled the effect. Since it did not have the desired impact, in 1861 the Germans began copying American clocks, including details such as the American eagle. The copying on these "Amerikaners" was so exact that the German and American clocks are today often confused with each other. In the end, the Germans did what they did best—went for quality. The Massivs were often taken for high-quality English clocks, and took a significant part of the English market.

Historically the story of nineteenth-century clockmaking is the story of nineteenth-century industry—the refusal of Britain to modernise and its tendency to rest on its laurels, the increasing inconsequence of France, especially after its overwhelming defeat by Prussia in the Franco-Prussian War, and the eagerness of the new superpowers Germany and the United States to embrace new technology and methodology.

Opposite: Two south German novelty clocks from Augsburg, one of the great centres of clockmaking and ingenious mechanical work. Although this type of clock is often called a 'mystery' clock, there is really not much mystery about it. The term 'mystery' should rightly apply only to a timepiece in which there is no connection between the time indicator (whether a dial or a pointer) and the movement.

Below: An eccentric nineteenth-century skeleton clock which is like looking through the bars of a cage in a zoo. It reminds us that the Victorians applied much of their time in using immense skills and know-how in making items that can only be described as grotesque. It is only at a second glance that what appears to be a large flower motif in the centre of the frame is in fact the dial.

CHAPTER FOUR

WATCHES AND PORTABLE-CLOCKS

The earliest watches were not carried in the pocket but were hung from a chain draped around the neck. They derive from the spring-driven no-pendulum table clock developed especially in Nuremberg and Augsberg. The earliest watch seems to have appeared around 1510 and was most likely spherical, though subsequent watches were drum-shaped. This was the rational shape for a timepiece, as the upper and lower parts of the drum provided strong protection. A pierced cover was fitted to protect the dial, ornately engraved as were the drum sides. Many of the early watches were provided with striking mechanisms (known as clock-watches) or alarms.

Opposite: A spectacular display of watches of various periods, including a classic watch of 1760 by Arnold, and a cameo-backed watch with pendant consisting of two further cameos in gilt frames, presented in chatelaine fashion with additional hooks. The backs of watches presented a wealth of opportunity, incorporating pearls or monograms, while the casing itself could be of semi-precious stone or enamelled.

Left: A gilt German drum watch with an alarm, and a pendant, made about 1580, about seventy years after the first watches made an appearance. The side of the drum is of an asymmetrical trellis type. Not being very accurate, only one hand was fitted.

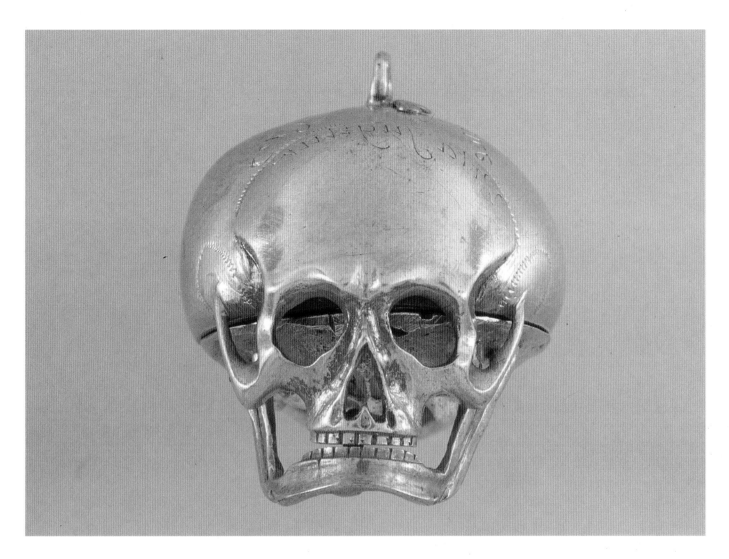

Seventeenth- and Eighteenth-Century Watches

Some time after 1610 watches became oval and twenty years later they more or less assumed the shape they have today. Glass was still not used as a dial cover; rock crystal was used instead, and the watch itself was often contained in a holder made of rock crystal or silver. During the seventeenth century watches assumed weird and irrational shapes such as skulls, crucifixes, stars, and seashells, and conventionally shaped watches were sometimes supplied with multiple cases, one inside the other, so that the mechanism was fully protected.

There was great competition between two great watch- and clockmakers, Daniel Quare (1649–1724) and Edward Barlow (born Edward Booth; 1639–1713) to gain royal approval and therefore guarantee their future success as creatures of the monarchy. The major clockmakers were prolific; Tompion alone produced 7,000 signed watches.

Great expertise was applied to the watch case, which might be engraved or enamelled, adorned with gold filigree or tortoiseshell, or dotted with silver pin heads protruding through leather to form a pattern. This technique of "dotting" was also used in pottery in the provinces, employing blobs of slip (liquid clay).

Dials were initially engraved but were later enamelled. At this stage the watch

Above: In the seventeenth century, when life expectancy was a good deal less than forty, time was a reminder of death and the brevity of life. This was particularly true in Germany. Skull watches, as well as watches dressed up as crucifixes, are evidence of this obsession, for it was not a functional way to make a timepiece, and the skull was not even a part of the movement, but an added extra. This example is by J. C. Wolf and the date would be about 1620.

Opposite: Silver watch of about 1650 with a pierced and engraved case of a high level of execution, featuring flowers and plant forms . The movement is by Jean Vallier of Lyons. By this time watches were assuming an orthodox shape, though they were still inaccurate and would remain so until 1675, when the balance hairspring revolutionised time-keeping.

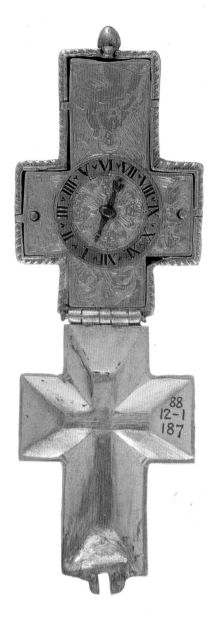

Above: Gilt hinged crucifix watch made by C. Tinelly of Aix and dating from about 1630. The gilt case is engraved with religious scenes. By the seventeenth century, brass had begun to be used for all parts of the movement except the steel arbors and pinions, clicks and springs, the mainspring, and the screws. The balance cock was ornately pierced and designed. In the 1960s, collecting them was so popular that watches well worth collecting in their own right were destroyed just for the sake of the balance cock, which, to add humiliation, was made into chic jewellery.

Left: James II gilt metal oval verge watch of about 1600. The verge escapement was used for more than five hundred years, even after the anchor escapement had theoretically rendered it obsolete. Its main asset was that it was simple and effective. The Germans had been supreme in the early years of the watch, but this example shows how the English watchmakers were moving on. The movement is by R. Whitwell.

was inaccurate and was not equipped with a minute hand. Only with the 1675 introduction of the balance spring—a thin, coiled spring—did the a minute hand appear, and minute marks, in multiples of five, were placed on the dial.

The functional watch therefore arrived very late on the clockmaking scene, though it had been adorned and cherished as if it had been an achievement of the highest order, as it was seen despite technical imperfections. Many early watches are known only by their appearance in paintings and illustrations, sharing a feature with early furniture that no longer exists, but it is clear that these watches were regarded with reverence and an awe that was often reserved for natural curiosities such as ostrich eggs, which were mounted in silver. English makers, regarding the overloading of surface decoration with suspicion, produced a much plainer version known as the Puritan watch.

Clockmaking and watchmaking did represent the cutting edge of new technology, but there was the additional appeal of miniaturisation, a characteristic that has an enduring fascination for the human race. But equipped with the right tools and good eyesight, a qualified craftsman has no problems working on a small scale.

As balance-spring watches came into vogue, a varied crop of unusual dials appeared. Between about 1690 and 1710 there were novelties such as the "wandering dial" in which an hour number moves across a semicircular minute scale from 0 to 60, disappearing on the right to be replaced by the next number appearing on the left. Since there were no hands and the dial surface was crammed with decoration, the time was difficult to read, making these items serve primarily as vehicles for watchmakers to show off their skills. Other watches have normal minute hands, with the hour shown in an aperture, a dial for a calender, one for adjustment, and an addition dial showing an oscillating disc, demonstrating the watch in motion.

Above: Tulip-shaped Dutch watch by Daniel van Pilcom from about 1640. It is no wonder that the tulip was selected as a case by the Dutch. The tulip was brought to western Europe from Turkey in the sixteenth century, found a natural home in Holland, and provided a good deal of wealth to this already immensely prosperous country. One tulip plant, the Viceroy, sold for the great sum of 4,203 guilders.

Left: An array of mostly silver pocket watches, primarily Victorian. The British could not compete in the mass market with the American watch factories, and even putting up tax on watch imports from the US failed to stem the flow. This was also true of American shelf clocks, which ultimately put the wooden clockmakers of Bavaria in serious difficulties.

Opposite: Enamelled gold watch which, with its picture of twin cobras, was possibly intended for the Indian market. The British Empire provided a major export opportunity for British timepieces, many of which were angled to particular interests. Often gadgetry was added (such as erotic automata), though the Swiss were eventually to be the dominating force in this area.

Opposite: Seventeenth-century gold and silver pocket watches of various dates (one watch has one hand, one has two). The gold watch is unusual in that the dial has an inner ring with additional numerals, making it a twenty-four hour watch.

Below: A rare astronomical watch by William Crayle of about 1660. The ingenuity displayed by watchmakers was staggering. By using a series of 'trains', the number of accessories and subsidiaries in what was apparently a straightforward watch could be endless, and governed only by the ability to miniaturise to the very limits.

This served in the same way as the aperture in a long-case clock—there is nothing so enticing as seeing the workings of a timepiece.

These so-called pendulum watches necessitated a good deal of ingenuity, and progress since the introduction of the balance wheel had occurred at a phenomenal rate. In less than twenty-five years, watches had evolved from somewhat useless prestige pieces to sophisticated artefacts, and with better escapements the modern watch was being born. Sometimes watch dials were made with an aperture in which a series of portraits and other pictures appeared at the whim of the viewer, totally unconnected with telling the time and no more than eye-grabbing gimmicks. Much the same was happening with the gadgetry added to long-case clocks. On some watches, pressing a pendant sounded the hours and quarters on an interior bell (the repeater).

With every available surface crammed with decoration, metal dials were, not surprisingly, found difficult to read, and a plainer enamel dial with a paucity of ornament was deemed vastly preferable. This was later exploited by the great French watchmakers such as Breguet.

The movement was hinged so that it folded out of the case, and the outer case was fastened with a spring catch, opened by pressing a raised button. Antique watches sometimes pose problems since the spring catches occasionally no longer work.

Above: A watch by J. Windmills from about 1700 (left) with an aperture depicting the sun and the moon, and signed in bold capitals rather than script. It is a well-conceived and unusual watch, as is the silver watch by Barraud of Cornhill, London, which has three dials: one for the hours, one for the minutes, and one for the seconds. It is, in fact, a nineteenth-century stopwatch.

One of the basic elements of the watch is a pierced and scrolled flat balance cock, roughly circular in shape with a prominent foot. It is here that applied ornament reaches its zenith, so much so that at a time when old watches were not collected they were simply smashed and the cocks were recovered and turned into jewellery in the form of brooches, bangles, and necklaces. The designs of cocks were not always purely ornamental but might depict animal and human faces.

Although balance cocks—which became larger with the introduction of the balance spring—were the most highly decorated parts of a watch, their makers were largely anonymous, though it is known that large numbers were made in Germany and Switzerland and imported for watches allegedly made by great makers. So little were watches appreciated in the 1960s that collages made of watch parts were displayed on velvet in glazed frames; they were especially popular in the Saturday antiques market in London's Portobello Road.

The verge escapement, or crown-wheel escapement (so called because it was shaped like a crown and was set at right angles) had been the mainstay of both clocks and watches since the earliest days, but in the pursuit of slimmer watches new escapements were being introduced, often not very different from their fellows. George Graham invented the cylinder escapement in 1726. Jewelling and the art of piercing rubies, sapphires, garnets, and crystal to reduce wear and help retain the oil was devised about 1704 but was not employed until much later, used to some extent by Graham from about 1725 onward. Graham is also credited with the evolution of the dust cover, often of gilded brass, which fitted snugly to keep out dust. The ultimate eighteenth-century watch was the pocket chronometer, the

Below: The caption on the previous photograph might well be repeated here, but these watches are by the great Swiss-born watchmaker, Abraham Louis Breguet (1747–1823), who moved to Paris in 1762. He evolved the self-winding watch and produced clocks of incredible complexity, including the pendule sympathetique, which was capable of automatically winding, correcting, and regulating a watch entrusted to its care overnight. Like the English genius of time-keeping, George Graham, Breguet was two hundred years ahead of his time.

Rolls-Royce of pocket watches, which confirmed Britain's supremacy in timekeeping. It was too sophisticated, complicated, and expensive to be produced commercially.

By the middle of the eighteenth century there was a general design consensus. Dials were plain white enamel, blued steel hands were restrained and clear, Roman numerals were used for the hours, and rather large Arabic numerals marked the five-minute intervals. The enamel was carefully applied in several layers and because of the glasslike quality they remain in virtually mint condition and only careless handling will cause them to crack.

The watch dials of this period are as aesthetically pleasing as the furniture and porcelain of the era—restrained, confident, and understated. The designs on the cases, heavily influenced by the Rococo movement, were carried out with great skill and taste. The subjects were often mythological, and the styles could include relief decoration (*repoussé,* meaning pushed from beneath) and coloured enamel. Because of natural wear and tear, watches with enamel cases were often provided with an extra carrying case.

Subsequent changes in watch movements were relatively inconspicuous, though decoration changed as the various fashions came and went. To cushion the inner case of pair-cased watches (double cases), a watch-paper was used. This advertised the maker or the retailer, and often any repairs were recorded on the watch-paper instead of being scratched on the inside of the case. Other watch furniture includes the winding keys, often art objects in themselves, sometimes made in the form of a crank.

Right: A fine collection of silver and enamel men's and ladies' timepieces.

French and Swiss Watches

Once again, makers were free to experiment because they were underpinned by the support of the king. As in mantel clocks, numerals on French watches were often set on enamel cartouches, and their cases were far more elaborate than those made in England. Exquisite art objects they may have been, but they did not need to compete in the market. At the same time, the French were producing the simplest and most beautiful watches of all time, purely functional and with movements of absolute perfection.

The leading watchmaker was Abraham Louis Breguet (1747–1823). If there was anyone to compare with Graham and Harrison it was he, prolific in the invention of increasingly sophisticated escapements and the inventor of the self-winding watch. His English agents tried in vain to persuade him to come to England. In 1802 Breguet received a gold medal at an exhibition of French industrial products for his "new constant-force free escapement." At a time when mass production was becoming viable he shunned it, numbering his individual creations.

In the late eighteenth century Breguet invented the carriage clock, a truly portable clock that served as an alternative to the watch. There were earlier unsuccessful and ugly forms in the shape of an outsize watch, but Breguet developed a small square clock in brass or gilt metal with a carrying handle for use by military

Opposite: A selection of frivolous novelty watches, a modern equivalent of the skulls and curios that ushered in the age of the watch. One supposes that they tell the time.

Below: The interior of a quite modern watch, a place of great mystery to many, as the inner workings are now often hidden from view by the small plates to which the mechanisms are affixed. Jewels were inserted where there were moving parts, and help to prevent wear. The fact that a watch is jewelled is of little consequence.

officers. It was first employed for this purpose by order of Napoleon in his Egyptian campaign of 1798.

Customarily kept in a leather carrying case, the carriage clock generally had glass sides, sometimes incorporating lavish ornamentation such as engraving and enamelled and porcelain panels in place of the glass. It might contain subsidiary dials, and a wide variety of alarm and striking mechanisms of a scale rarely achieved in other timekeepers, such as the *grande sonnerie* mechanism. Its most important quality was its shockproof movement. The item may be seen as a miniature skeleton clock, with the movement shown in action. The balance and escapement are at the top of the movement rather than on the back plate.

Carriage clocks were made in various sizes and were sometimes oval. The smaller the size, the more desirable to collectors. Until about 1820 most carriage clocks were made in France, but they proved so popular that they were made in quantity by all the clockmaking countries, not as portable timepieces but because they were trim and neat, invariably had easily read dials, and were ideal for ladies' boudoirs. It is doubtful whether they were used by many officers or saw a shot fired in anger. The carriage clock survived almost unchanged until about 1910, when it fell into decline, only to be taken up with enthusiasm half a century later. But technically the style was a dead end. Watches had supplanted the need for portable clocks, attractive as they may have bee

Toward the end of the eighteenth century Arabic numerals were first used on watches for the hours, for some time a feature of French timepieces. There was a good deal of interaction between the European clockmaking countries, and the duplex escapement by the French maker Pierre le Roy was introduced

to Britain by Thomas Tyrer in 1782. The lever escapement, which proved the most suitable for commercial watches, was first made by Thomas Mudge in 1770. However, the verge escapement continued to be made well into the nineteenth century because of its simplicity of construction, its reliability, and the ease with which provincial clockmakers could effect a repair. Inventors could be too clever by half.

The Swiss were entering the scene as major players, providing fine movements for the English market. The film *The Third Man* contemptuously declared that the Swiss accomplished nothing more than the development of the cuckoo clock, but their powers of invention reached far beyond that. They demonstrated great skills in such gadgetry as automata, musical movements, and incredibly complex mechanisms such as singing birds, which arose from the body of the watch through miniature trapdoors. The "singing" was operated by tiny bellows and a swanee whistle. In miniaturisation the Swiss were supreme. Their musical watch operated on the same principle as a cylinder musical box, with the music provided by a comb of tuned teeth "sounded" by pins on a minute revolving cylinder.

Keyless winding for watches was patented in 1814. Yet this was not the self-winding watch that had already been invented by Breguet; it was a useless novelty whereby a pendant was pumped up and down with the thumb.

Throughout the nineteenth century the watch, almost alone, remained virtually unchanged in shape or basic mechanism. Because silver was cheap, even mundane watches had silver cases. The best known of these were Hunters (all silver) and half-Hunters (with an small aperture in the top so that the time could be seen without opening the case).

American Developments in Watchmaking

Instead of inventing new escapements, watchmakers were more concerned with satisfying the demand and seeing off the competition. This was done by subcontracting; "rough movements" or *ébauches* were made by local and provincial makers and finished off elsewhere, the most important centre being Coventry. But without the principle of interchangeable parts that marked the American industry's dominance (in clockmaking as in other fields), mass production faltered against the competition of the United States.

American watchmaking had been virtually nonexistent in the eighteenth century, and those that do bear American names are actually English "rough movements" refined in the United States. The most important developments occurred in Connecticut. Thomas Harland (1735–1807) was producing about two hundred home-grown movements a year in 1802. Through changes of personnel from about 1851, the American Horologe Company became the Boston Watch Company, and then Howard and Dennison, high-class makers. There were first-rate American watchmakers, such as E. Howard. The Railroad Watch of about 1907 was a superb precision instrument, the equal of any watch in the world.

The ultimate American mass-produced watch was the Waterbury, made of only

Opposite: Five fine pocket watches. Almost unique amongst timepieces, the pocket watch retained its form throughout the nineteenth century. The watch on the upper right is from 1857 and has a patented movement by G. Fasoldt. The watch on the bottom left is a pocket chronometer.

Below: The term 'fob watch' is meaningless, and is often given to a lady's watch, or a small watch. Watches were, of course, wound by a key, which was attached to a 'fob', and worn with a watch on a man's waistcoat or front trouser pocket. Many keys were of splendid quality, often 'cranked' like a car handle. Breguet introduced the 'tipsy' key, which prevented the owner from winding the watch backwards when drunk.

fifty-eight components and first produced in 1878. With a duplex escapement and a spring nine feet long it took an inordinate amount of time to wind, but at $3.50 (at a time when there were five dollars to the pound sterling) it was worth it. Waterbury and the other major companies, many now based in Massachusetts, were each producing in excess of 300,000 watches as year.

No British firm could even begin to compete with such a coup, which turned traditional watchmaking on its head. Although the American mass-production watch world was one of bankruptcy, triumph, setback, and doggedness, it exported on such a scale that the British watch industry was ruined. A Lancashire firm tried to emulate the Americans, but long-held traditions and practices led to its abject failure. America and Germany had overtaken Britain as the workshops of the world; Britain was in terminal decline.

The Wristwatch

Originally made for officers of the German Navy, wristwatches were at first called wristlets. They were greeted with derision when they appeared in Britain about 1880. Dust, humidity, or jerky arm movements would damage the movements, and men dared not wear them since wristwatches were considered effeminate.

Wristwatches became compulsory for officers in World War I. The dials were shielded by metal, or, instead of glass (since it could shatter dangerously), celluloid was substituted, which either burst into flames or contracted in the cold and fell out. Luminous dials were invented about 1915.

Rolex (originally Wilsdorf and Davies) was one of the earliest firms, introducing the Rolex "Oyster" in 1926. The Rolex self-winding watch arrived in 1931, though it was not a new invention. Early watches had the winding mechanism above the twelve. In the 1920s and 1930s, unusual luxury watches proliferated; they shared the fact that they were difficult to read, with numerals replaced by marks or even left out altogether. The first alarm wristwatch dates from 1892 but it was not a success.

Opposite: A Breguet watch bearing the inscription 'Breguet et Fils', which indicates that it is after 1807, when he took his son into the business. It is accompanied by its leather carrying case. From the invoice it appears that the watch has a duplex escapement, described as one in which the escape wheel has both spur and crown teeth, traditionally attributed to the French watchmaker Pierre le Roy in 1750. The escapement is the device by which the power of a timepiece is transmitted to a pendulum or balance, and the technical details of the hundreds of variations are of concern only to specialists.

Left: The individual craftsman was replaced by mass production in Switzerland in 1865 by Roskopf, and in 1880 the Waterbury Company began production for a worldwide market. Ingersoll is also one of the key watch factories, and the interior of this, the firm's first watch, is in stark contrast to the refiinement of watchmaker pieces. It is stark, and there is no attempt at sophistication or subtlety; it is a machine rather than a work of art.

CHAPTER FIVE

MODERN TIMEPIECES

The first tentative attempts to use electricity for timekeeping actually date back to 1834 and resulted in a viable clock as early as 1842. Several types of electric clock were exhibited in the Great Exhibition of 1851, and in 1852 an electric clock with four illuminated dials was set up for some time in front of the Electric Telegraph Company office in the Strand, London. But widespread use of electricity in clockmaking did not occur until the twentieth century, when it proved the industry's most important technical advance in the century.

The Electric Clock

Electricity was first provided by battery. Early electric clocks worked on the principle of an electromagnetically impulsed pendulum, but by replacing the pendulum with a conventional but large balance, an unwieldy piece of apparatus was made more compact. But batteries were cumbersome affairs and, since battery voltage varied, the early electric clocks were not very good timekeepers.

Opposite: A selection of ladies' watches with fine enamelling: at bottom right, a modern watch by Vacheron and Constantin with a mixture of numbers and abstract symbols on the dial, two Rolex wristwatches, and a pair of Mickey Mouse timepieces. Rolex, one of the greatest names in wristwatches, carried on the great watchmakers' tradition of being understated in their designs. The quality lay within.

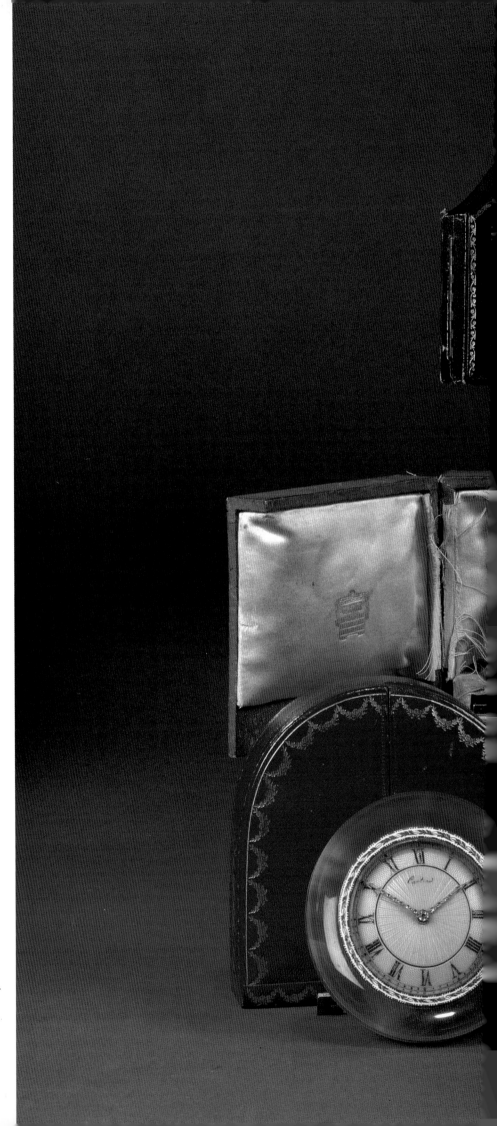

Previous page: Dunhill's introduced small watches into the sides of their lighters during the Art Deco period, but they were a short-lived novelty in an age that thrived on unusual to bizarre treatments. These included a long-case clock design with a cocktail cabinet in the trunk of the clock, and tennis balls that opened up to reveal an ash trays. Although there were fine makers, more attention went into presentation than into the quality of the movements. By the turn of the century all timepieces were reasonably accurate, and few were greatly concerned with a minute or two lost or gained in a day.

Right: Cartier portable timepieces in an extraordinary range of styles, from the bizarre half-moon clock in the background that seems to echo the half-arches of the classic long-case clock, through the modernistic rectangular clock , to the circular clocks in the foreground. The rectangular clock is the most powerful. Dials had been square, round and oval, but innovative designers of the 1920s and especially the 1930s saw no reason why a rectangular dial should not be made. Art Deco was suitable for marble, malachite, onyx, and other natural materials, and these were used without compunction in association with precious and semi-precious stones, metal (silvered bronze being a favourite), and plastic, which did not have the down-market implications it now has.

Above; The watch stand has a long pedigree, having been made in almost all materials, including pottery, wood, and most metals, but this is one of the most ingenious, incorporating a bracket with a hook from which to hang the watch, a tilting magnifying glass on a stand, and a small electric bulb activated by a press-button switch.

Opposite: If there is one man to rank with Christopher Dresser as a designer two generations ahead of his time, it was Charles Rennie Mackintosh (1868–1928). Best known for his architecture, his masterpiece being the Glasgow School of Art (1897), he was also active in many other fields, ranging from furniture to cutlery. Spare and often angular, his work is also influenced by Celtic motifs, as in the hands of this ebonised clock with inlaid decoration: functional, stark and effective.

The Americans were leaders in electric clocks. The Eureka clock, invented in 1906, had a plain dial of quite ordinary appearance with a movement behind; these were fixed on a wooden box that contained the battery. In 1910 Thomas Murday of Brighton, Sussex, developed an electric clock with a horizontal movement, instead of vertical as in the Eureka. Both the clocks were housed under glass domes with their movements fully exposed, the modern equivalent of the skeleton clock. Electricity was a great mystery, so electric clocks—functionally inferior to almost all other timepieces of the period—had novelty value.

A curious feature of electric clocks was that they were often left skeletonised and there was no attempt to encase them. They were regarded as inventors' toys or scientific instruments without commercial appeal, and they did not have the decorative potential to appeal to the general public, who were perfectly well provided with conventional clocks. Eureka electric clocks were sometimes provided with elegant mahogany cases that matched Edwardian furniture.

A pendulum clock, the Electric Regulator, was patented by Percival Bentley in 1910, and was commercially produced by his Earth Driven Clock Company of Leicester. Perhaps the greatest name in pioneer electric clocks is William Shortt (1882–1971), who produced a pendulum clock accurate to one or two thousands of a second per day. The Shortt Free Pendulum Clock was used as the standard at

Above: A truly remarkable timepiece. It could be described as a skeleton clock, though the intentions of the clockmaker are a mystery.

Right: A marvellous collection of carriage clocks and small table clocks. The carriage clocks are at the highest end of the market, with enamelling of superlative quality. They are a long way from the early days of the carriage clock, invented as a portable leather-cased timepiece for military officers.

Greenwich Observatory from 1925 until 1942. It might be said to have been the most accurate clock in the world.

Clockmakers hated electric clocks. They could see their industry slipping away from them just as they had come to terms with the threat of American, German, and more recently Swiss imports. Switzerland was gradually assuming a prominence in high-quality timepieces, especially watches.

The most disliked clocks were the gaudy and extravagant High Victorian clocks, especially those at the cheap end of the market. Yet it would be wrong to reject all these out of hand; a good deal of ingenuity and invention was present in the more expensive ones. Perhaps the most disagreeable are the pottery clocks, with transfer-print decoration. Throughout the Edwardian period and long beyond the classic bracket clock continued to be made in considerable quantities, though often the dimensions were awkward and details such as the handle could be mean. They sported a wide variety of finishes, including green lacquer, mahogany with mother-of-pearl and brass inlay, and walnut. Some latter-day bracket clocks were fitted with Westminster chimes.

Clocks belong to the class of antiques owned by ordinary people for whom the timepiece may be the only old thing in the house, and they are regularly handed down from generation to generation. This accounts for the large number of Victorian mantel clocks still available at exceptionally modest prices, much less than they originally cost if inflation is taken into account.

Opposite: Pewter was one the favourite materials of the Art Nouveau period. Although it may not be to everyone's taste, this clock has many adventurous features, including the innovative design of the numbers, the curious red blobs on the green dial, and the insertion of enamel globules into the body of the clock. The decoration on the pewter consists of stylised flower forms. The most famous pewter was 'Tudric', sold by Liberty's and far less eccentric.

Below: Metallic Art Deco clock face with decoration consisting of geometric shapes, and the dial flanked by two chimpanzee heads. The maker is 'Just'. Just what?

Art Clocks

The Arts and Crafts movement of the late nineteenth century had seen timid expeditions into clock design, but its rugged and rustic ethos was anathema to clockmaking—a denial of industry. Had the Arts and Crafts practitioners been asked, they would probably have deemed a sandglass more aesthetically acceptable.

The styling of Art Nouveau proved much more amenable to clock design. The movement of clocks of the Art Nouveau period was unimportant; it was the look that counted. Designs followed those in other applied arts of the time. French clocks were sinuous; they often had the texture of melting wax, and whiplash motifs were a popular feature. English clocks were inclined to be more angular, with eccentric detail. Wood, no longer the predominant material, vied with silver, pewter, and other metals and alloys.

French timepieces in particular had a tendency to frivolity. In their pendulettes the pendulum, swinging in an open frame beneath a broad, leaf-shaped dial, might have a grotesque face with grinning teeth as the bob. Numbers were often in curious, difficult-to-read, self-consciously amusing styles, or they might be replaced by letters spelling out mottoes that happened to have twelve letters. So *Tempus fugit* ("Time flies") was out while *Festina lente* ("Make haste slowly") was in. This favourite device of English clockcase makers reflected the enthusiasm of furniture makers for adding mottoes to their furniture and the earnestness of interior designers who inscribed life-enhancing mottoes on beams and on walls.

Well-known designers were involved in clock case design, including C. F. A. Voysey (1857–1941), a follower of William Morris and a believer in traditional methods. His clock case of 1906 resembles a four-tiered building with ball feet,

Opposite: A splendid Art Deco mystery clock with an architectural pediment made of rock crystal, mother-of-pearl, and other stone, with diamond chips used for the numbers and set into the hands. 1930s mystery clocks of this quality have recently been reproduced in Switzerland, without the impudence of replacing the clockwork movement with quartz.

Below: A rare solution to the problem of the portable clock was a wristwatch in a flat hinge-lid case, attached to the wrist by a tassle. It would obviously be a handbag watch if there were such a term.

Above: A black marble/slate clock of modest quality with the curious addition of green stones.

starkly modern but handmade of ebony and oak, with pegged joints (always a sign of superior craftsmanship). Voysey apparently could not make up his mind what style of numerals to use and in the end seems to have picked the wrong one. G. G. Elmslie, who worked for the American architect Louis Sullivan (1856–1924), embraced a muted modernism in his long-case clock of 1912, using mahogany with brass inlay, a pierced and irrelevant Celtic cross in the centre of the trunk, and odd-shaped pillars projecting above the top of the case with ugly capping.

Some of these objects demonstrate the folly of being forward-looking without knowing what to be looking forward to. At least the French Art Nouveau artists operated in a milieu they understood. English clocks of the years preceding World War I usually took their tone from the eighteenth-century revival mahogany and

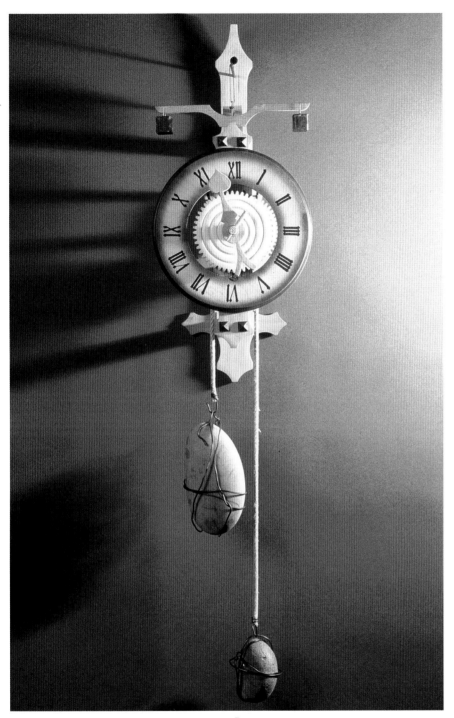

Above: Like all other fields, time-keeping has its eccentricities. This do-it-yourself-style watch stand was thought interesting enough to be photographed, and may have its admirers.

satinwood furniture that was fashionable, and outnumbered "advanced" design by a factor of at least twenty to one. Unostentatious and unglamorous, these clocks have retained their quiet desirability. The balloon clock with a pinched-in waist was particularly popular.

Twentieth-Century Clocks

Novelty clocks enjoyed a revival from about 1910 onward. The gravity clock was a round dial movement that used its own weight to drive it down two parallel brass pillars. When it needed winding the clock was simply hauled to the top of the pil-

lars. The torsion pendulum clock has a flat round horizontal pendulum, and the power is very slowly released as the pendulum oscillates from side to side. It can go for a year on one winding. The digital or ticket clock, hardly more than a piece of nonsense, resembles the old-fashioned steel desk calenders where the days and dates revolve on a drum. It has a simple clockwork mechanism that, instead of activating hands on a dial, flicks a "ticket" as each minute goes by. The case was curiously in the form of a carriage clock.

The 1925 decorative arts exhibition in Paris, which heralded the Jazz Age, was a spur to designers of all kinds, not least to those who provided the settings for clock and watch movements. Little happened to the movements—mechanical timekeeping had reached its limit except in miniaturisation (resulting in the cocktail watch). The dial itself was often the least important feature in the streamlined glitzy concoctions, incorporating the fashionable reworkings of Aztec, Geometric, Egyptian, Russian Ballet, Cubist, and Inca themes in all kinds of materials, often together. Silvered bronze and onyx were a popular combination. There was no reluctance to use brightly coloured plastics in combination with precious and semiprecious metals.

The French and the Americans—such as Kem Weber (1889–1963), responsible for the splendid streamlined Zephyr digital watch of about 1933—were among the most adventurous. The Art Deco stylists had a description for their creations— "beautility." Many of the clocks were what would have been exhibition pieces considered in the nineteenth century, made for self-advertisement, too expensive to be

Opposite: A classical Art Nouveau pewter clock by Liberty, which has all the innovation and none of the eccentricity of the period, with a flat canted top, a nicely modelled trunk, and charming squat feet, while the blue enamelling of the dial is a good foil to the soft silver-grey of pewter, one of the most appealing of alloys.

Left: A 1920s silver lady's watch of some charm. Despite its popularity, Art Deco had only a limited effect on everyday life. Textiles, pottery, furniture, and carpets in a modified chainstore-Deco style were popular amongst the general public, but Deco art objects were not as common. Watches, avant garde ceramics, and the novelties which intrigued the cafe set were largely ignored or simply not known. Without the cinema and the influence of Hollywood, Art Deco would have been the province of a small coterie.

Nicole, Nielsen & Cº
14 Soho Square,
London.

made commercially, self-indulgent dead ends. Jean Goulden created Cubist clocks of staggering beauty using silvered bronze, enamel, and marble, but since his total output was no more than a hundred and fifty different pieces including clocks, his work would have been too expensive for all but the very rich.

Some Art Deco clocks were fun-pieces, hardly claiming to be great art. These include Jaeger le Coultre's stirrup-shaped clocks with gilded wood frame, red leather dial, and numerals composed of plain blocks of gilt metal. Cartier's "mystery clock" of 1921 in the Egyptian style has no mystery about it except why it was made; it has all the appeal of a seaside trinket. The "clocktail cabinet" is ostensibly a square-dialled long-case clock, but the door opens to reveal shelves for bottles, glasses, and soda syphons and a rack inside the door for swizzle sticks.

The powder compact with a watch set in the lid may have proved a talking point—once. Table watches—miniature clocks usually hinged from side uprights—served little purpose except as dressing-table nicknacks. Watches surrounded by diamond clusters have all the appeal of Victorian paste jewellery, available at any junk stall at a thousandth of the cost.

Among the most appealing products of the 1930s are the commercial spin-offs from Art Deco, such as the cream plastic alarm clocks with stepped sides made by

Opposite: A silver grande-sonnerie (grand-sounding) striking clock with carrying handle and subsidiary dials by Nicole Nielson of London dating from the early years of the twentieth century. A timepiece of the highest quality and of some refinement it reflects the subtle changes in taste that had been taking place since the 1870s.

Left: Highly distinctive gold, enamel, and pearl Art Nouveau watch, with the enamel inset between ridges of metal, a reflection of the cloisonné technique used in classical enamelling. The technique is different in that the enamel is not poured into the containers in liquid form.

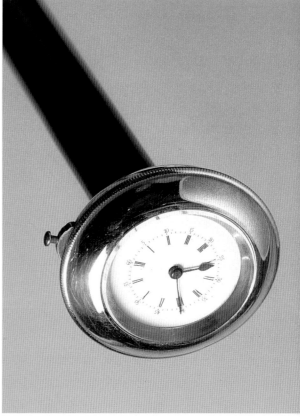

Left: The most famous watch in the world, the Rolex Oyster. First produced in 1926, it incorporated a self-sealing winding crown, which made the watch waterproof. This was why it was called the Oyster.

Ingersoll in the United Kingdom, the self-consciously modernist clocks that avid cinemagoers had seen on the movies and wanted to possess themselves—the brash and the bright that enlightened the gloom of many a suburban house. The most characteristic 1930s clock was the "sunburst" clock, but it was heavily outnumbered in the average home by the oak silvered-dial mantel clock with chimes. Millions of these were made, and millions are still sold; there seems no end of them in antique shops and on flea-market stalls.

Of course there are "deserving cases," the austere fitness-for-purpose clocks that owe more to the Bauhaus than Art Deco, but there are far too many near-misses. The green onyx clock surmounted by *The Bat Dancer* in ivory and bronze by F. Preiss is valuable by virtue of the figure. The clock is a disagreeable, cheap-looking movement set in a commonplace, sharply stepped surround. Rock crystal, jade, and obsidian—three of the rare favourite materials—provide little interest if misapplied.

Clock and watch technology, to all intents and purposes, had reached the end of the road. Although there was a modest revival of the streamlining and straight-line vogue in the 1950s for the commercial market, there was no question that never again would clock design be of much aesthetic interest. Quartz clocks and watches had given timekeeping accuracy to millions for no more than £1.95 ($3).

Classic clocks were among the earliest antiques to be taken up for use rather than show, but among the discerning they have never gone out of fashion.

Above: Watch affixed to the end of a cane for a reason that was, no doubt, viable.

Opposite: Rock-crystal Art Deco clock by Cartier. The crown and crossed monograms on the plinth may indicate that it was a royal commission.

Overleaf: Attractive watch in a realistic 1930s setting, reflecting the time when a pocket watch was worn with pride on a waistcoat front, especially if it was silver. For the poor or lower middle class it was a prestige symbol, a token that one had made some progress up the social scale. The pocket watch unquestionably belongs to the age of the cuff link and the collar stud and is gone forever.

INDEX

PICTURE CREDITS

Ancient Art and Architecture Collection
8, 10 (left & right), 11, 12, 13, 14,15, 16–17

The Bridgeman Art Library, London
26, 34, 35, 36, 37, 38, 42, 43 (left), 44, 45, 46, 47 (right),
59, 60 , 61, 64, 68, 69, 79, 82, 83, 84, 85, 87 (right), 89 (right), 90, 91,
92, 93 (left), 103, 104, 109, 112, 117, 118, 120, 122, 123 (left)

Christie's Images
6, 7, 18, 19 (left), 20, 21, 22, 23 (left & right), 25–25,
27, 30, 31, 35 (right), 42 (right), 48, 49, 50, 51, 52–53,
56, 62–63, 67, 70, 71, 73, 74–75, 80, 86/87, 96, 99 (top), 100,
102, 106–107, 110–111, 115, 121, 124–125

Images Colour Library
32

MC Picture Library
19 (right), 28 (left), 28–29, 39, 40, 41, 43 (right),
47 (left), 54, 57, 58, 62 (left), 65, 66 (top & bottom),
72, 74 (left), 76, 81, 88, 89 (left), 94–95, 97, 101, 105,
108, 114, 116, 117 (right), 119, 123 (right)

Ronald Pearsall
33, 55, 93 (right), 98, 110 (left), 113

The Wright Family Collection
77, 78, 99 (bottom)